Break the Cycle!

Other books by Arend Ardon (in Dutch):

Klantgestuurde teams
Veranderen spiegelen aan anderen
Ontketen vernieuwing

Arend Ardon

Break the Cycle!

How managers block change without realizing it

Warden Press

To Bram and Ruth

© 2018 Arend Ardon

ISBN:
Paperback: 978-94-92004-62-8
E-book (Epub): 978-94-92004-63-5
E-book (Kindle): 978-94-92004-64-2

Original title: *Doorbreek de cirkel! Hoe managers onbewust verandering blokkeren* (Amsterdam: Business Contact, 2011 / 2017 [18th edition]). Translated from the Dutch by Erwin Postma.
Cover design: Studio Kers, Rotterdam
Interior design and lay-out: Bert Holtkamp, Groningen
Photo author: Frank Groeliken, Zaandam

This edition published by Warden Press, Amsterdam

wardenpress.com

Table of contents

Preface

You'll only see it when you get it

Ever been on a winter driving course where you were taught skid recovery techniques? The number one rule in a skid: lay off the brakes! Hitting the brakes will only make the skid worse. I remember one conversation I had with my instructor about that big red light on the dashboard.

> Me: 'What's that red light for?' Instructor: 'It will light up when you hit the brakes.'
> Me: 'But surely I'll know when I've hit the brakes?' Instructor: 'You probably won't.'
> Me: 'I find that hard to believe. Besides, I won't be applying the brakes anyway, you've just taught me not to.'
> Instructor: 'Just drive...'

I remember I got into a skid and made two 360-degree turns. The red light came on ...

> Me: 'But I didn't even brake.'
> Instructor: 'You thought you weren't going to and you think you didn't. That's what the red light is for.'

I found this absolutely fascinating. I had basically hit the brakes unknowingly. And that while I had so firmly resolved not to. It was a reflex: I saw danger, so I applied the brakes. Instead of keeping me safe, my subconscious self-preservation ended up putting me in danger...

Years later, I would regularly encounter similar situations in the corporate world. At many companies and organizations that engaged me as a consultant, I would find a typical manager who wanted an open and honest culture at his department, where people can speak their minds, where every opinion counts, and where managers therefore must show an interest and ask questions. And this manager would really mean all of this. But whenever discussions at a meeting would get heated, he would still go out of his way to convince others they were wrong. Result: others would just give in to be done with it and think twice about expressing their opinion next time. The manager was not aware of his behavior. If only there had been a big red light on the meeting room table...

The more I was asked to breathe new life into change processes that had gone stale, the more examples I encountered of these kinds of fascinating situations. Managers with top-notch change management expertise who knew exactly how managers should act, but who still saw their change processes come to nothing. They would all work with the best of intentions to steer the process in the right direction but end up with unwanted outcomes. This was because they would, without realizing it, do exactly those things that cause change processes to fail.

Given that we are not aware of how our actions lead to change processes grinding to a halt, we do not address them at management meetings. Instead, we talk about milestone plans and change strategies that will help us change the process and the employees. But as we discuss plans, we do things that have the power to make or break the change process. And we do them without realizing it.

Wanting to get to the bottom of this, I dedicated four years of postgraduate research to this phenomenon, attending around 100 meetings, ranging from board meetings to management team meetings and regular team meetings, and keeping an accurate log of what was said and what happened at those meetings, ultimately totaling around 1,700 pages of notes. I also spoke to managers personally to tune in to their thinking. The next step was to analyze all my notes, tracking down recurring patterns, identifying thought processes, and studying management behavior. It opened up a whole new world to me!

Without realizing it:
- we have counterproductive assumptions about change processes
- we don't do as we say
- we display behavior that makes employees dependent and reactive
- we undermine employees' entrepreneurial spirit and sense of responsibility
- we tackle recurring problems with the same approach every time, and
- we try to block discussion of our own ineffectiveness.

If you listen closely and look at what is going on in the here and now, you will obtain a wealth of information about how change processes end up stagnating. It is a learning curve. You will not see it right away, because all those 'suspicious' comments and behaviors initially seem so logical and familiar. And because we view them through the same glasses that caused the problems in the first place.

This book will help you understand why change processes stagnate. And, even more importantly, how you are one of the main reasons why they stagnate. This book will help you become aware of your subconscious assumptions and behavior, and make you see the unwanted effects. It will show you how you are keeping the vicious cycle going and how the same problems keep coming back. The emphasis in this book is not on providing tips and tricks, but rather on helping you understand how you are the one perpetuating difficult situations. By analyzing your own behavior and approach, you will learn to breathe new life into your stale change processes.

This book is structured along the lines of the six basic principles of breaking the cycle and achieving real change.

Break the Cycle! - The Six Principles

1. *Recognize persistent situations*
   Sometimes the problem and the solution are crystal clear. When that happens, you 'only' have to intervene. But in sticky situations, intervening often only makes things worse. That is when you need an understanding of how you are perpetuating the problem through the way you think and act. The question is how to recognize these kinds of situations.
2. *Be aware of your thinking about change*
   Without realizing it, you have all kinds of assumptions about how change processes work. These assumptions are often

based on the idea that you, as the manager, can simply 'implement' change. Your choices are based on these assumptions, and so they can get you into serious trouble. You can, however, breathe new life into change processes by rethinking your assumptions.

3. *See what you do when the going gets tough*

   The key to successful change lies in the here and now, in what happens between you and others in day-to-day interactions. You know how important it is to get your employees involved in the decision-making process, how important it is to listen to them, and how important it is to get to the bottom of their concerns. But chances are that, when push comes to shove, you lose sight of all that. This is because when the going gets tough, our autopilot tends to take over. Without realizing it, we unilaterally try to stay in control of the situation, thus undermining the change process. If you are aware of this happening, you can override your autopilot and switch back to manual mode.

4. *Understand how you are perpetuating the situation*

   Whenever changes are not going smoothly, you sometimes feel you are going around in circles. And you probably are. It is very likely that you and your people have indeed ended up in a vicious cycle that has you all running in a kind of hamster wheel. All you are doing is perpetuating the current situation. But you can stop the hamster wheel.

5. *Dare to discuss the undiscussable*

   Learning happens when you openly address the effectiveness of your actions. The thing is, however, that we are not very good at that. We often try to sweep information about our own ineffectiveness under the rug, using so-called defensive strategies, which are very logical and inconspicuous. This is how we ultimately block learning and change. Talking about it and getting it out in the open has turned out to be a very effective way of unblocking it.

6. *Start small*

We talk about change a lot, and we are quick to set up all kinds of projects. But real change is realized only when you manage to create an open communication climate in which everyone, including you, learns from the things that happen. A transparent guideline will give you something to go by in putting this into practice.

Every chapter is structured in the same way.

• *Real-life example*

An explicit fragment of a management team discussion or a conversation between a manager and their staff is used to illustrate the subject covered in the chapter. These exchanges are taken from a company where management wants to realize culture change to make employees more enterprising and more result-driven. At first glance, the exchanges may seem very normal. It all seems so logical...

• *What is actually happening?*

The chapter will help you understand what is actually happening. And how those seemingly logical exchanges show how we, without realizing it, are making change processes grind to a halt, undermining people's sense of responsibility, and causing recurring problems. A combination of real-life examples and new insights.

• *How to breathe new life into a situation*

Targeted suggestions will help you break deadlocks, generally by openly discussing the situation, openly addressing your own role, and exploring new ways together.

- *Breakthroughs*
  In every chapter, you will find 'breakthroughs', which are exercises for you to do in your own day-to-day work to put insights from this book into practice. The emphasis of these exercises is often on boosting your understanding of your own role in any sticky situations that you may find yourself in at work. These interventions have all been tried and tested in real-life environments, and they have proven their effectiveness.
- *The essence*
  Every chapter closes with a brief recap of the essence of what was covered in the chapter in four or five bullet points.

The headers in the chapters are not exact copies of those listed above, as that would make things boring. But you will instantly recognize the line of thought they represent in each chapter.

This book is based on my PhD thesis entitled *Moving Moments*. In working on my thesis and this book, I have drawn inspiration from a number of authors, with Chris Argyris being my main source of inspiration. He has written a great deal about the inconsistency between what managers say and what they do. Peter Senge's work shows beautifully how we inadvertently perpetuate problems. Bill Noonan and Diana McLain Smith have managed to make Argyris' often difficult-to-read works more accessible. Check the back of this book for a list of books worth reading by these and several other authors. What all these books have in common is that they do not try to present change processes as customizable step-by-step plans. Instead, they all try to get to the bottom of what really happens. Although that is indeed a more complex undertaking, it is ten times more exciting than the misleading simplicity of 'do it this way and it will all work out fine.'

This book is about managers and where they hit a wall. Managers are not a special breed of people with out of the ordinary behavioral tendencies. This book deals with human behavior, albeit shown by managers in specific situations in the context of change processes.

The challenge for me in writing this book was to capture years of scientific research in a book with actual practical relevance. I hope that you, after reading it, conclude that I have succeeded in doing that. And I hope that this book will help you realize how we, through seemingly normal and rational behavior, are causing our change processes to fail. You'll only see it when you get it.

1 Recognize persistent situations

Be in the picture

'We have to push them hard.'

> Manager 1: 'Remember we discussed in the beginning that the new structure also had to lead to different behavior? Enterprising employees, result-driven attitude...'
>
> Director: 'You want to do too much too quickly. We are focusing on the structure first. We'll deal with the culture later.'
>
> Manager 1: 'But how can you see these as two separate things? To be able to organize work processes properly, employees are really going to have to show more initiative. We still have to push them hard...'
>
> Manager 2: 'You've got a point there. The employees themselves lack drive. We keep having to convince them to act. Sometimes I feel we're going around in circles.'
>
> Manager 1: 'I don't want them to do it for me, I want them to do it of their own accord.'
>
> Director: 'Also in the future, we are going to need initiative and entrepreneurial spirit. Assign responsibilities lower down in the organization. That's where we are going to have to launch a culture-change process.'

These managers feel they have to push their employees hard. They try to convince employees and do their utmost to propel them into action. But they are not getting anywhere. They feel they are going around in circles. The director suggests tackling the culture. But the question is whether that is the solution. This chapter will show that it will probably not lead to much of anything, simply because it is a solution that was chosen without knowing the problem. It is an intervention that is not based on understanding. In this chapter, you will read all about how difficult change situations call for a unique approach, and about how to recognize persistent situations.

Recurring difficulties

I am often engaged by companies that have been trying to realize change for some time, without ever achieving satisfactory results. Interventions produce short-lived improvements, but the same symptoms always reappear after some time. Examples of such persistent situations are poor customer satisfaction or a lack of entrepreneurial spirit across the company. In a strikingly large number of cases, managers claim that employees are overly reactive, have too much of a wait-and-see attitude, and are even cynical. Employees, in turn, describe the corporate culture as threatening and the management as directive.

Common examples of persistent situations include when you try to boost your people's sense of initiative, but they stick with their wait-and-see approach. Or you do your utmost to garner support for your plans, but your employees keep resisting. Sometimes it seems as if the harder you try, the more difficult it gets. Despite your best intentions, the meetings, and the workshops, you feel you are not getting anywhere. The same problems keep coming back. The change process stagnates.

When things get difficult and your best intentions do not lead to improvement: stop! You are only wasting your time. Initiatives that may seem logical will only take you from bad to worse. More of the same will only get you into trouble. These persistent situations call for an entirely different approach. But the question is how to recognize them.

Gunshot wounds and excess weight

When it comes to identifying persistent situations, we can learn a thing or two from doctors. They distinguish between acute and persistent symptoms all the time. Obvious examples of acute conditions are a gunshot wound or a broken leg. With these kinds of injuries, the problem and the solution are crystal clear. The doctor knows what is good for you and will assume all responsibility for your treatment. As the patient, you submit yourself to your doctor's intervention without challenging it. You relinquish your responsibility and become dependent.

But what about when you are overweight, and diets and exercise have not produced any weight loss, or when you suffer from chronic headaches or stress? Both the problem and the solution are a lot less self-evident in those cases. A painkiller will alleviate the headache, but only for a short while. In the long term, a painkiller is a solution that may even worsen the problem. After all, the underlying problem could be stress, which, in turn, is caused by an inability to handle pressure. If these underlying issues are not tackled, the headaches will keep coming back in the long term. By taking a painkiller, you have only temporarily bypassed the real problem. And the real problem may even have gotten worse in the process, as symptoms were suppressed by the pill and the patient starts to feel dependent on the doctor.

The same kind of dichotomy applies to organizational problems. There are cases when the problem is clear and the solution obvious. For example, when waiting times rise due to understaffing, the solution is to (temporarily) hire additional staff. And when the information system does not return the right management information, the system needs to be reconfigured.

In other cases, the problem and the solution are not as clear-cut. If your employees are insufficiently enterprising, you can offer them a workshop (much like a pill) that will teach them to be more enterprising. This might spur them on, but it could also worsen the problem. Their reactive attitude may be the result of the fact that managers keep organizing things for them, such as workshops, and they barely ever have to take responsibility themselves.

So, you can basically distinguish two kinds of situations:

1. *straightforward situations* with a clear problem and a clear solution. In such situations, the required action is self-evident. It is as clear-cut as dressing a gunshot wound;
2. *persistent situations* where seemingly logical solutions do not produce logical results. Well-intended initiatives may only make the situation worse. Problems keep coming back, it is all very troublesome, you are not making any progress.

This book is about persistent situations. The emphasis in such situations should be on understanding instead of on intervening: how did we get here, how am I perpetuating it?

Take the persistent situation where efforts to make employees more enterprising keep failing. Instead of devising an approach to boost employees' entrepreneurial spirit, it would be far more useful to first understand why employees are not enterprising in the first place. How are we causing employees to adopt a passive wait-and-see attitude?

Breakthrough 1

Which persistent situations do you recognize?

You can recognize persistent situations by the fact that they consume a lot of your energy, while the initiatives you take to resolve them yield little. These situations make you feel all knotted up inside and they create tension. You have doubts about the approach, because your previous initiatives failed.

Below you will find a list of several common persistent situations. Check the boxes for the ones you have faced in your working life.

- ❑ You have been trying to motivate your people to take more initiative and be more enterprising, but you are not getting anywhere.
- ❑ You have made several attempts to bridge the gap between management and staff, but your attempts have come to nothing.
- ❑ You keep trying to break down the resistance to change, but you only seem to accomplish the opposite.
- ❑ You do your utmost to motivate and inspire your staff, but they simply seem to lack any kind of drive.
- ❑ You have taken a range of initiatives to raise employee satisfaction, but the scores continue to be low.

❏   You communicate until you're blue in the face, but they are
    still unhappy about communications about change.
❏   You feel that you are being very clear on the need for
    change, but they are just not accepting it.
❏   People keep saying 'yes' but doing 'no'.
❏   …

Now write down what is making the situations you have
selected so persistent. What causes the process to stall and the
problem to persist?

From intervention to understanding

To recognize persistent situations, you need to learn to look and
listen very closely. If you do that, you will see how you, despite
having the best of intentions, are basically reinforcing the current
situation. Go back and carefully read the management team discussion at the start of this chapter again. The managers say a couple of things that can be classed as 'suspicious' in this context. But
they are not aware of it. They are in the middle of the situation.
Do you recognize these 'suspicious' statements?

A few examples:

✗ 'They are really going to have to show more initiative. We still
   have to push them hard.' And: 'The employees themselves lack
   drive. We keep having to convince them to act.'
   It seems that these managers think that persuading and pushing their employees will help them get more out of their
   employees. But they have already seen that it does not work,

so why do they keep doing it? And what could be the effect of all that convincing? It might just backfire.

✗ 'I don't want them to do it for me, I want them to do it of their own accord.'
Very understandable. This is something that I hear a lot. But it is also basically an impossible task: I don't want you to do it for me, I want you to do of your own accord. It is the same as telling someone to be spontaneous.

✗ 'We are going to have to launch a culture-change process.'
Are they really going to launch a culture-change process to make employees more enterprising? That could prove tricky with all that convincing and pushing by managers going on. Chances are employees will only become more reactive.

These kinds of statements taken from real-life situations may seem rational and quite innocent, but they contain a lot of information about the root cause of the difficulties: managers' thinking and behavior. The most important starting point for a process of real change lies in managers themselves.

We are often more tuned in to what others do than in to what we do ourselves. Especially when things get challenging, we tend to resort to behavior that is counterproductive. And due to these counterproductive effects, the situation only becomes more challenging to us. This leads to recurring patterns that can we can get wrapped up in, while not realizing that we are actually the ones perpetuating these patterns. Others do realize it, but generally say nothing. This leads to very strange situations: everyone is sick of the difficulties, everyone feels their intentions are good, everyone is frustrated about others not seeing it, and meanwhile we keep talking about change strategies. And we keep trying to come up with ways to get things under control again, using progress indicators, scorecards, and step-by-step plans. More of the same and therefore never achieving real change. Lots of intervening, little understanding.

Make sure you are in the picture

Going back to the exchanges from the above management team discussion, there is something else that stands out. The talk is all about culture change, but no mention is made of changes to the managers' own behavior. It is as if they are not part of the culture they consider so undesirable. They are basically taking a picture of the situation without being in it themselves. They are safely stood behind the camera. No wonder that they are so hands-off in how they talk about changing others through workshops. There is no way change can succeed in this way.

This is a common situation that I often encounter at companies. Although we talk about how to contribute to change, such as by organizing meetings or offering support, it often does not go further than a vague and hands-off 'solution approach': the managers are behind the camera, manning the controls for the employees who need to change. But all this talk does not address the question of 'how we have contributed to making the situation what it is today?' The challenge is therefore to be in the picture of the situation. Only then will you see how you are part of the situation and how you will have to change to change the situation. The best question you can ask yourself is this: *how is their behavior down to me?*

I once used this picture metaphor when presenting my diagnosis at a company. The situation at that company had become rather grim. Trust between management and (highly-qualified) professionals had reached a new low. Communications were difficult. After interviewing several people at the company, I shared my findings. My message to this company boiled down to this: 'No one I spoke to included themselves in the picture. Nobody saw themselves as part of the problem. And that is the problem. If you want to help make improvements, you have to be in the picture of the situation (in other words: if you are not part of the solution, you are part of the problem). Would you be willing to go along with this?'

After a moment of silence, the janitor rose to his feet and yelled out: 'So that's basically a selfie!' I thought this was a brilliant remark. It captures a basic precondition: you need to be able to take a lighthearted and frank look at the situation and at yourself in that situation. And this happens to be something we often struggle with, especially in challenging situations. I asked the janitor whether I could quote him. He consented, on the condition that I also mention his profession. That would, in his view, be a nice boost for janitors everywhere. Consider it done…

Breakthrough 2

How to be in the picture

In breakthrough 1, you selected persistent situations that you have seen in your day-to-day work. And you identified the reasons why these situations keep happening.

Now take another close look at the causes you have identified and answer the two questions below. Make sure you are in the picture of the situation, as in a situational selfie, and try to be uninhibited and keep a little bit of distance from the lens.

1. How often did you consider others the main cause of the problem? And how often did you name yourself as the possible cause? Weigh your answers on the scales below and see what happens.

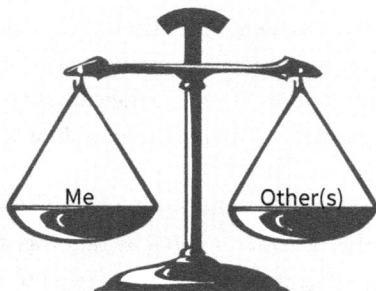

Me   Other(s)

2. Try to tip the scales towards your side. What could be your role in perpetuating the persistent situation?

By answering these questions, you are taking that much-needed situational selfie. Each of the next breakthroughs will gradually turn your situational selfie into a sharper picture of the situation.

This book will show how persistent situations arise and how you are probably the one perpetuating them through your approach to change processes, your way of thinking, and, more than anything else, your behavior. As soon as you see and understand this, improvement of the situation will be within reach.

Recognize persistent situations

1. *When things get difficult and your best intentions do not lead to improvement: stop!*
2. *More of the same will only get you into more trouble.*
3. *You've got no time to lose, so take time to explore how the same problems keep recurring.*
4. *Take a situational selfie: how are you subconsciously perpetuating problems?*

2

Be aware of your thinking about change

Stagnation of change begins in your mind

'How do we go about rolling out the new culture?'

Director: 'Okay, people, the culture-change process…'

HR manager: 'Look, culture change is the single most difficult thing to achieve. We have to put it in concrete terms for the people. Many companies have core values. We agreed upon entrepreneurship, result-driven attitude, and personal responsibility. But we have to get people involved to create broad support.'

Manager 1: 'The key question is, in my view, how to roll out these values. How do we get employees to really take responsibility? Is training an option? One way or another, they have to get familiarized with the culture.'

HR manager: 'We first need to discuss the core values with a small group of employees to see whether they buy into them, and then we can organize training programs. At the end of each training, participants will have to formulate personal actions to put the core values into practice.'

Director: 'That sounds like a good plan to me.'

Manager 2: 'I wonder how people will respond to this. Cynically, I fear.'

Director: 'Exactly, and that cynicism is precisely the problem we want to eradicate. But we need a good backstory. We have to explain the need behind the culture change, that we will not survive without it. People need to be more enterprising, more innovative.'

How do we go about rolling out the new culture? And how do we get employees to truly take responsibility? These are questions that show how managers think about change. Perhaps there is something else that strikes you about these exchanges. This chapter will show how erroneous assumptions about change lead to choices that backfire. Be aware of your thinking about change.

Implement, introduce, or roll out?

We constantly implement all kinds of things at our companies, such as a new structure, a new budgeting method, or new software. But we also think we can implement performance management, a different culture, or core values. I keep hearing the term 'roll out' a lot these days, as in 'We are going to roll out new values.' Financial institutions around the world are busy implementing integrity. And one young, passionate manager recently asked me to help him 'boost' the new result-driven culture at his organization. This way of talking about change implies a firm belief that change can be forged. And it is precisely this belief that turns out to be a precursor to difficulties, sticky situations, cynicism, and energy loss.

Why are we so eager to implement? Many books on change management are based on the implementation mindset: management comes up with a change idea and subsequently implements it through a nicely phased plan. The well-known formula of $E = Q \times A$ (Effectiveness equals Quality times Acceptance) is an example of this. As managers, you feel it is up to you to come up with a sound plan, which you then (only) have to get accepted. This way of thinking has taken root at companies in a big way. It is logical and ties in seamlessly with the idea that everything can be engineered. But we are oblivious to the fact that this thinking produces unwanted effects, because we are not aware of our assumptions. Common (subconscious) assumptions 'hidden' in the implementation mindset are:

✗ Change is realized through management initiatives; we do not expect employees to change of their own accord.
✗ Management has the capacity to change employees by using the right methods. Management can change their working methods, their behavior, and even their (personal) values.
✗ As employees are generally reticent to change, management must put them under pressure by, for example, using compelling arguments to stress the need for change.
✗ Employees will always resist change, meaning that managers need pre-prepared strategies to break down that resistance (such as by first being flexible and giving in, only to then return to the change you wanted all along. Treating employees as if they were one card shy of a full deck. But you will get away with that only once).
✗ As soon as they see an opportunity, employees will return to their old ways, so management will have to closely monitor progress.

This mindset says a lot about how we view the manager-employee relationship: the manager takes the initiative, the employee reacts. The manager comes up with a change, to which the employee subsequently submits. The manager is active, the employee dependent. I often refer to this as 'box thinking': employees are like unwitting boxes waiting passively for the manager to move them. Things get painful when management subsequently becomes aware of employees' inactive attitude and decides that employees' sense of initiative needs to be strengthened: preferably through a new step-by-step plan.

The transparency test

Is it a bad thing to subconsciously use such assumptions? Let's look at the impact it has. I sometimes have managers do the so-called transparency test, which I borrowed from American researcher Roger Schwarz. Here's how it goes: imagine you were to make your assumptions explicit (which means you first have to be aware of them) and be completely candid about everything, what would happen? It would mean that you would tell your employees the following: 'Dear staff, given that you never take any change initiatives, we, as the management, have come up with yet another initiative to change you. We realize that you are not fond of change, and we have therefore already thought of ways to put you under pressure to change. And since you are bound to resist the change, we have also already worked out how to break down your resistance. As we do not think you will actively engage with the change, we will be closely monitoring progress.'

How would your employees react to that? Probably not with great enthusiasm. You will alienate them, they will adopt a passive and perhaps even cynical attitude, they will feel belittled or not taken seriously. But what if you do not make these kinds of assumptions explicit but subconsciously let them drive your approach anyway? What would the chances be that your employees sense that you think that way and still react as described above...?

This is precisely the risk that comes with the implementation mindset. Without realizing it, we have assumptions, design our approach based on these assumptions, and the outcome we get is a confirmation of these assumptions (and therefore of our approach). We keep the loop closed for ourselves and keep doing what we have always been doing. And all the while we are claiming that we want change. The term 'implementation' alone conjures up a number of compelling images: it imposes something that comes from the outside, something that currently does not exist, something people do not know and cannot do, something about which people are uninformed. The more your employees hear that word bandied about, the more they will start behaving with an attitude of 'we'll see what they come up with next.' This kind of passive wait-and-see attitude is what management takes as 'resistance', and often even as additional confirmation that it really is about time that they 'implement' a culture change. All in all, it is hard work for all parties, whereby these parties mainly work against each other. It is basically a case of a vicious cycle, or a self-fulfilling prophecy: the harder you 'implement', the more reluctant your employees become, the harder you will 'implement' again...

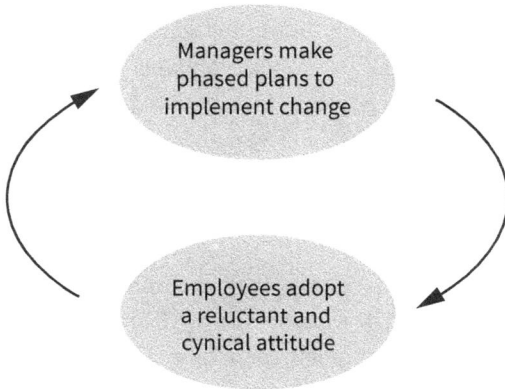

Breakthrough 3

How do you approach the change process?

In the table on the next page, indicate to what extent your change approach is based on the (implicit) assumptions listed. Add up your scores. If the sum of your scores is higher than 15 points, your change approach is based strongly on the implementation mindset. A perfectly fine approach for structures and systems, but one with major pitfalls when it comes to changing behavior, attitude, and working and collaboration methods. You should realize that this approach reinforces a culture where employees will adopt a reliant, reluctant, and even cynical attitude. Or they will fight you. If you want to create a culture where employees take initiative and responsibility, this approach will be counterproductive: you will basically end up reinforcing the culture you have set out to change

	to a very small degree	to a small degree	to a rea-sonable degree	to a large degree	to a very large degree
1. Real change is realized on the initiative of management.	1	2	3	4	5
2. To activate employees, management has to increase the pressure.	1	2	3	4	5
3. With the right methods, management can change employees or their behavior.	1	2	3	4	5
4. With the right strategies, employees' resistance to change can be broken down.	1	2	3	4	5
5. If management does not keep a close eye on progress, employees will return to their old ways.	1	2	3	4	5

Combating inconsistency

Our thinking creates inconsistency. The assumptions that underlie the implementation mindset drive our approach in change processes. This approach is often, without us realizing it, at odds with the outcome we want to achieve. Here's an example.

Customer focus

Management wants to change the culture at the company: the focus has to be on customers. They want all existing teams, headed up by their respective team leaders, to come up with points for improvement and put these into practice. This initially triggers a decent number of improvement initiatives, but one year later it has all died down again. Team leaders and managers complain about how difficult the situation is. No wonder, because the culture has not changed in any way. The culture is that people obediently do what they are asked or told to do and show little initiative. The approach is entirely in keeping with this culture: management asks for points for improvement and the employees deliver. Employees will only keep delivering potential improvements if management keeps asking for it.

In short: a good approach when you want to temporarily make a few improvements, but it will never yield lasting change. To realize lasting change, the way of working must be called into question: why does management feel they have to get employees to come up with potential improvements? How does management undermine the sense of initiative and entrepreneurial spirit of their own people?

Here are another couple of examples, taken from real life.

Anonymous 360° feedback

To promote a climate of open learning, one company decided to introduce a 360° feedback system. Managers, a few customers, peers, and employees were all asked to write down their impression of a certain individual on a special form. Anonymously, so that everyone would write what they really thought. But by going down this route of anonymous feedback, they were not actually helping to create a climate of open learning. On the contrary, this measure reinforced the existing culture: 'since we cannot handle honest information, we'll do it anonymously.' It would have been more consistent with the actual objective behind introducing the feedback system to openly exchange feedback in face-to-face conversations, perhaps with an objective moderator present.

Boosting employee satisfaction

In another example, a company's annual (anonymous) employee satisfaction survey once again returned a low score on commitment to the company. Employees' primary complaint: tasks, authorizations, and responsibilities are unclear. Like in previous years, board members responded with a knee-jerk reaction, trying to resolve the complaint right away. The HR department was asked to make clear descriptions of tasks, authorizations, and responsibilities for all jobs. A year later, the score is even lower than before. As bewildering as it may be, there is an explanation for it. Employees evidently do not feel committed to the company. An employee satisfaction survey is utilitarian and impersonal. A confirmation of reality. Managers instantly get to work on solving the alleged problem; they want to eliminate it. Well-intentioned, but also perpetuating the pattern of reliant employees who identify problems and managers who immediately start solving them. Commitment is more likely to be created through a conversation, through contact.

The interventions ensue from the same thought process that caused the problems in the first place. More of the same. As long as we keep thinking in the same way, we will keep doing the same things, and create the same problems. Or, in the words of Einstein: 'The significant problems we have cannot be solved at the same level of thinking we were at when we created them.'

Breakthrough 4

How (in)consistent are you?

We are all inconsistent all the time. There is no need to be ashamed of that. That said, it can considerably undermine the effectiveness of your change efforts. It is therefore useful to keep checking your approach for consistency with the goals you have set yourself.

Think of a change process that is particularly tough-going. Then look at the figure on the next page and answer these four questions:

1. Change goal: what do you want to achieve with the change process?
2. Change approach: what are the main features of the change approach?
3. (Side) effects: what are the positive or adverse effects of the chosen approach?
    Take a critical look at points such as:
    – employees' sense of commitment

- relationship of dependency between superior and employees (as in the vicious cycle)
- your employees' / co-workers' sense of initiative and responsibility
- your level of trust in your employees / co-workers
- their trust in you
- the relationship between you and your employees / co-workers.

4. (In)consistency: to what degree do the effects match the change goal you are pursuing?

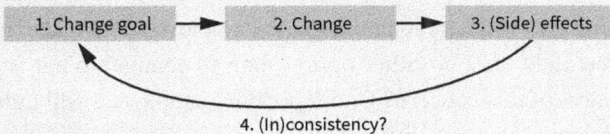

From rolling out to figuring out

From rolling out to figuring out

Let's go back to the management team meeting that opened this chapter. Where do you recognize the implementation mindset? And can you see how this mindset jeopardizes the intended change right from the start?

Let me highlight a few statements.

✗ 'The key question is, in my view, how to roll out these values. How do we get employees to truly take responsibility?'
Rolling out an entrepreneurial spirit and sense of responsibility? Consider this from the point of view of the employee who

is told that a sense of personal responsibility will be rolled out on him or her. This is bound to backfire.

✗ 'We need a clear step-by-step plan, otherwise it is all bound to be too vague.'

Although there is nothing wrong with having a step-by-step plan, it does sound like a controlled way to implement new behavior.

✗ 'And at the end of every training session, participants have to formulate personal actions.'

Where does this comment come from? Is this manager worried that employees will otherwise do nothing? Does he think that they will have to pressurize the employees and make them feel they have no other option than to change? What is the effect of this concern? Under pressure, employees will indeed formulate actions, but how likely are they to actually execute them? Change then becomes conditional on management exerting constant pressure. *Change?*

✗ Manager: 'Cynically, I fear.' Director: 'Exactly, and that cynicism is precisely the problem we want to eradicate.'

This is a fine example of circular reasoning: our approach makes our people cynical, and we take this cynicism as confirmation that we must intervene.

✗ 'We need a good backstory to explain the need behind the culture change, that we won't survive without it.'

The underlying need for the change has to be clear, that goes without saying. But a watertight backstory may also suppress any kind of interaction (although that might actually be what these managers want).

This management team meeting is an accurate illustration of the implementation mindset. The people in charge are used to implementing things. This, in turn, has encouraged employees to adopt an increasingly reluctant, passive, and even cynical attitude, instead of becoming more enterprising and taking initiative and responsibility. They simply opt to wait and see what the next management initiative will be, knowing that one will always come. And such an initiative will again try to ignite employees' entrepreneurial spirit and sense of initiative, in the same top-down implementation manner that ultimately only undermines these very qualities. And when this initiative makes people even more unassertive, the director takes that as proof that a culture change is needed.

Episodic change and continuous change

Is the implementation approach 'wrong'? No, it is unilateral. It is a highly functional approach when you need to implement structures or systems. 'On date x we will be switching to the new system.' The actual switch will come after months of communication and training, but it will actually happen on the scheduled date. That is when the new system goes live. Some employees will maintain that they preferred the old or another system, but the new system is what it is and they cannot do anything about that. This kind of change is easy to plan, realize, and even enforceable, if necessary. For example, the balanced scorecard is something you can implement for technology and working methods. Better employee performance, on the other hand, is not something you can implement.

With change projects that target behavior, attitude, and ways of working or innovating together, assumptions resulting from the implementation mindset soon lead to inconsistency. Those kinds of changes call for a different way of thinking. They call for a different perspective. I refer to this perspective as 'continuous change.' When you assume a perspective of continuous change, you will see that changes are not realized only on the initiative of managers.

If we open our eyes, we will see that employees are actually constantly busy making small changes. They come up with ideas, make suggestions, and raise objections to the usual ways of working. Not as part of an episodic change project but rather in a continuous process of changing and learning. Managers can stimulate this process, but they can also undermine it (through top-down implementation of one change after the other).

Continuous change is based on very different assumptions than the implementation mindset.

✗ Employees constantly make small changes to their work practices. They are right-minded people who like doing a good job. Consecutive changes imposed by management undermine such initiatives, as they make employees reactive instead of proactive.

✗ In the best-case scenario, putting pressure on employees will make them submissive and passive. Employees do not need to be put under pressure to change, they just want to understand what problem is being tackled or what improvement is targeted.

✗ Management has the capacity to stimulate innovation and improvement by removing obstacles, exploring new ways, and figuring out together why some initiatives keep failing. Less 'this is how it is' and more 'I don't know either, let's try it together.'

✗ Employees want to be taken seriously; they have valuable information that can enrich and may contradict the information management has. It is up to the manager and the employees to solve this jigsaw puzzle of pieces of information together.

✗ If employees see that their input adds value, they will not try 'to get out of it.' They enjoy it when the value they add is noticed and appreciated.

This process of learning and changing is a constant process, but it is also constantly obstructed. These obstructions arise in day-to-day interactions between managers, between managers and employees, and between employees. When you talk change, this process of learning and changing is ongoing between you and others.

They sometimes seem like two separate worlds that exist side by side.

1. The world of change plans and approaches, of change and stagnation.
2. And the world of day-to-day interactions that conduce either to change and learning or to recurring problems. This is what really happens.

The respective perspectives of these worlds open your eyes to different things. The below table shows these differences. In putting together this table, I drew inspiration from Karl Weick and Robert Quinn, whose contributions in this area are, in my view, nothing short of groundbreaking.

Episodic change (implementation approach)	Continuous change and learning
What we talk about	What really happens
Change is episodic and initiated by managers	Change and learning happens continuously and everywhere
Emphasis on implementation	Emphasis on learning
Change = to correct 'flaws' in structures and systems	Changing and learning = to understand how we create recurring problems and obstructions ourselves and to learn how to eliminate them
Systems and structures	Behavior, collaboration, interaction
Macro level: step-by-step plans and change strategies	Micro level: day-to-day interactions
There and then	Here and now
Rolling out on a large scale	Figuring out on a small scale
Intervene	Understand
'This is how it is…'	'I don't know either, let's try it together.'
Management charts the path	The path is created by walking it
How do we change the structure, implement a different performance assessment system, or roll out a new working method?	How do we energize people, trigger creativity, stimulate a sense of responsibility and an entrepreneurial spirit, and boost teamwork?

There is plenty of management literature about the left column. We are relatively good at all of that. We are tuned in to the jargon of the implementation mindset, and step-by-step plans give us something to lean on. Although harder to put into practice, the right-hand column has great impact on a company's or department's capacity to set up successful change processes together. Especially when change processes prove tough-going, focus on the right-hand column. There is a great deal to discover there!

The key lies in the here and now

My research shows that change success is shaped largely in day-to-day interactions between managers and between managers and their employees. As you discuss a change project with your employees, the behavior you display in the here and now will either boost or block the change process. In other words, regardless of the change approach you pick, your behavior is what determines whether there will be real change. In our interactions, we often create recurring problems and (unwittingly) allow the process to stall. Culture is what we do while we talk about diagnosing organizational problems and realizing culture change.

If you feel that your employees are not enterprising or innovative enough, you can try to change them through step-by-step plans and smart interventions. From the top down, without engaging with employees, as if you were not part of the company (culture). However, this has not proven very effective in practice. At best, it leads to a cosmetic change: we turn everything upside down, but only reinforce what we already have. What would happen if you were to switch your focus from the there and then to the here and now? If you would not talk about passive employees and how hard it is to change them, but instead ask how they have come to be that way. How did they become what they are today at your company?

The answer to this question often lies in the here and now. Take a step back and really look and listen to realize how you, the managers, talk to each other. Are you in the habit of coming up with lots of changes for your employees? Do you feel that you always have to take the initiative? Do you often talk about how to garner support for your ideas? If so, you might already have the answer to the question why employees are so passive...

Breakthrough 5

How is your behavior contributing to the current unwanted situation?

When a process proves tough-going, you can get your people together and introduce new step-by-step plans, measuring tools, and progress meetings to improve the situation. But that is likely to just be more of the same. Instead, you should first try to understand the current situation. Your way of thinking and handling the situation has obviously not produced the outcome you were after. So, what exactly does your way look like? Engage with each other by asking the following questions.

- ✗ What exactly is the problem we are coming up against in the current situation?
- ✗ How are our approach and behavior creating that problem? How are we perpetuating the problem?
- ✗ How is their behavior down to us?
- ✗ How do we discuss the change process?

✗ To what extent do we tend to talk about the behavior of our employees and 'the culture' as if they have nothing to do with our behavior?

✗ How do we apparently think about the change process?

✗ To what extent do we consider it a matter of rolling out something new?

✗ What are the (unwanted) effects of that?

✗ How does our approach to change undermine their initiative, commitment, and innovation capacity?

✗ To what extent do we try to move them around as if they were unknowing boxes? What effect does that have?

✗ What is your main conclusion? And what will be your next step?

Especially when a process is slowly grinding to a halt, you are coming up to the limit of the implementation approach. That is when your focus should shift from step-by-step plans and interventions to the interactions that obstruct the process of change and learning. Look at what really happens.

Be aware of your thinking about change

1. *Your assumptions about change drive your approach. Be aware of your assumptions; your approach might just be inconsistent with what you want to achieve.*

2. *If you think that only you can initiate change and that employees will always resist and do not want to change, you will eventually be right.*

3. *Structures and systems can be implemented, but behavior, attitude, and ways of working (together) cannot, these are things that people have to learn together.*

4. *And when it gets difficult, you should not resort to new step-by-step plans and interventions. Instead, look at interactions between you and others in the here and now: that's where you'll find the key.*

3

See what you do when the going gets tough

The manager's autopilot

'How do I stay in control?'

> Manager (as he wraps up a presentation to his team): ' …and that's why we have to bolster our customer focus.'
> Employee: 'But do you think this will work?'
> Manager: 'Sure, why wouldn't it?'
> Employee: 'We already spend a lot of time with customers. I regularly get compliments for our services.'
> Manager: 'But to be able to survive in the long term, we have to keep innovating. We have to keep surprising our customers.'
> Employee: 'I actually think we do not need to surprise our customers. They like us because they get exactly what they want. Without fuss and smooth talking.'
> Manager: 'But surely, there is always room for improvement in our customer focus, isn't there?'
> Employee (as he shrugs his shoulders): 'Yes.'
> Manager: 'Any further questions?'
> No questions.

In the end, the employee gives in, replying 'yes' when asked whether there is room for improvement. But is that a sincere 'yes', or a 'yes' just to be done with it because he does not want to get into a discussion with the manager? Change processes often get stuck in these little interactions between managers and their staff. That is where it all happens! Without realizing it, we try very hard to keep the situation under control. But we end up undermining the change process that way. If you can see how you get caught up in this cycle, you will come away with an entirely different approach to change processes. And you will see another way...

What we say ≠ what we do

Before the meeting from which the above real-life example was taken, I spoke to the manager involved. I asked him what he wanted to achieve at the meeting. His answer was a common one in these circles: 'commitment'. Then I asked him how he would be using his behavior to boost commitment. His answer came straight from popular management literature: I will be open to questions and concerns, keep asking questions, I won't go on the defensive, and I will keep an eye out for non-verbal signals. Fantastic! But at the meeting, his actual behavior was very different.

Afterwards, he said he was reasonably happy with how the meeting went. I reminded him that he wanted to boost commitment, asking him whether he thought he had succeeded. He thought he had. Even that one employee from the above fragment eventually came around to his way of thinking, everyone had said 'yes' in the end. But was it truly about (internal) commitment for him, or did he simply want everyone to agree with him, say 'yes', regardless of what they really thought? After a moment of hesitation, he said it was really all about commitment for him. I asked him whether he thought that last employee was now really more committed? He was not sure. Why didn't he ask the employee? His response to this question did not come as a surprise to me: what if the employee would have answered 'no' and others would have agreed with him?

That would have created a tricky situation. True, but the meeting would then have been about real sentiments and opinions. Now employees have said 'yes', but they will probably do 'no'. Whenever you come across this phenomenon in practice, you should really be asking yourself this: 'Why would people say 'yes' to me when they think 'no'? In what way could this be down to my behavior?'

What stands out here is that the manager's actual behavior at the meeting differs drastically from the behavior he, when asked in his office before the meeting, claimed he would be displaying. He is certainly not alone in this respect. What we say and what we do when it really matters are often two entirely different things. Typical lines that roll off the tongue with great ease but are very hard to put into practice are 'it's okay to make mistakes', 'we are open and fair', 'we will adopt a learning attitude', 'we create commitment', and 'we encourage entrepreneurial spirit, personal responsibility, and proactive behavior'.

Here are some more examples of inconsistency between words and behavior:

More innovation and creativity

One company has the ambition to be more innovative and creative, and presents this ambition in a policy plan, various slide presentations, and leaflets. However, in daily practice, the company's management team generally goes with whatever the majority wants. Members with different ideas without majority backing are always persuaded that they are wrong. The same thing happens deeper down in the organization.

An open and fair culture
Another company has come up with new core values. One of these is to be 'open and fair': we are open towards each other about what is on our mind and do not hold back in sharing our vision with stakeholders. However, when employees openly express an opinion that turns out to be inconvenient, managers brush it aside as being resistance and ignore the inconvenient information.

Responsibilities low down in the organization
A third company has concluded that it cannot be run by managers alone. People must take ownership and be accountable, also deeper down in the organization. In practice, however, strict progress reviews based on scorecards are managers' chosen method to keep things under control, making it hard for employees to take ownership.

Especially when things get difficult and tense, our behavior becomes more detached from our knowledge and intentions. But if our behavior is not driven by what we claim to find important, what is driving it? This is an exciting question!

Our autopilot controls our behavior
According to Chris Argyris, who was professor at Harvard Business School, our behavior is controlled by our basic survival instinct. What do you do when something is thrown at you? You

duck, evade, put your arms up or protect yourself in some other way. When facing a threat, you defend yourself. *You do it without thinking about it. Your autopilot takes over.*

Let's say you introduce a well-thought-out change idea to your employees. But then you sense among your staff that they are critical of your idea and do not understand it. We often, without realizing it, experience such situations as threatening. Your approach may be rejected, it could lead to loss of face, or you can lose control of the situation. And so you go on the defensive. *You do it without thinking about it. Your autopilot takes over.*

Especially when things get tense, our autopilot kicks in. Without us realizing it, our autopilot drives our behavior with one basic instruction: make sure you stay in control! And to stay in control, we do the following:

- we take our assumptions as the truth and do not challenge or test them: 'The employees resist change.'
- we try to convince others of our vision; increase the pressure by using (abstract) arguments such as: 'Surely you understand that our current approach is becoming less effective. The market is changing, and we have to change with it!'
- we turn the other cheek to inconvenient information and take other opinions as a sign of ignorance and unwillingness: 'He just doesn't want to understand.'
- we block any kind of discussion of inconvenient information (as that might blow holes in our reasoning or reveal mistakes we made).
- we talk in abstract terms (conclusions and commonplaces) and do not share the reasoning that got us to our conclusion:

'It is clear that the world is changing. We must increase our capacity for innovation.'

A key feature of the autopilot: we don't realize we are activating it. Others do notice, but they will not tell us.

Take another look at the conversation transcribed at the start of this chapter. Let me again highlight a few statements from it.

✗ Employee: 'But do you think this will work?' Manager: 'Sure, why wouldn't it?'
  The employee asks a question, but he is basically expressing an opinion. The manager replies with a counter-question. But the counter-question is not intended to really understand the question, but rather to convince (and win over) the employee.
✗ Manager: 'But surely, there is always room for improvement in our customer focus, isn't there?'
  Employee (as he shrugs his shoulders): 'Yes.'

It is hard to reply to such a platitude. The manager has succeeded in this situation, for now. He has stayed in control of it. But what this 'yes' from the employee is really worth will only be revealed when the time for action comes...

Standing on the sidelines, it is easy to analyze this kind of conversation. But when you are in the middle of it, you act before you realize what you are actually doing. I once organized a leadership and change day at a company. At this event, I explained the principle of the autopilot.

As I explained it, one of the participants spoke up and said that he had a different take on the idea of the autopilot. Although he did recognize some of the managers at his company in my description of the autopilot, he claimed that most acted differently from what I described. A few seconds later, I myself was slipping into autopilot mode, because I was trying to convince him my theory was correct. Why? Because I was afraid I was losing control of the situation. He had become a threat to me. His input was going to create an inconvenient situation, so I thought. I had to salvage the situation somehow. When I realized what I was doing, I decided to address it head on with the group: 'See, I'm doing it myself now.' I asked the participant in question what effect my trying to convince him was having on him. He replied that he felt pressurized. He felt that I didn't want any input from him. He said that he was inclined to say 'yes' to me, while thinking 'no.' And he finished by saying that the whole thing had discouraged him from getting actively involved. These are the unwanted side effects I had produced through my behavior. And that while I was explaining this very phenomenon!

I am rational, the other is wrong

The autopilot not only controls our behavior, it also determines how we view the situation. It takes over your judgment. My research confirms Argyris' theory of how we think when a situation becomes difficult, threatening, or embarrassing. In the following section, you will find the ten most common thoughts that people have in these kinds of situations. Before you delve into that list, it would be advisable to read breakthrough 6 first.

Breakthrough 6

How does your thinking lead to the situation becoming an uphill struggle?

Think back to a recent situation or talk where you did not achieve what you had set out to achieve, where you met with resistance, had a difference of opinion, or ended up in a conflict. A situation where you felt that you were not getting anywhere or going around in circles. Write down what you thought about the situation, about the other person involved, and about yourself in that situation. Only continue reading once you have done that. Now look at the ten thoughts people have in situations where they are unilaterally trying to stay in control of the situation. How many of these thoughts did you have? Find out what your score means below.

1-3 thoughts	You did not give in to your autopilot; the situation probably looks a lot better now.
4-6 thoughts	This is the average score. Keep reading to find out how to get things moving again.
7-10 thoughts	Your autopilot is fully operational, so the situation is probably fairly stuck.

Think about the consequences these thoughts are having on the situation. What is your assessment of the outcome? You will probably not be very pleased. And that while you undoubtedly did not set out to generate adverse effects. In summary: your intentions are good and without realizing it, you let your autopilot produce negative outcomes. Fascinating, isn't it?

Ten thoughts that go with unilateral management: how do I stay in control?

1. I am rational in my actions and my intentions are good.
2. I am right.
3. I must stay in control.
4. The other is wrong.
5. The other acts out of self-interest and has bad intentions.
6. The other makes little effort to listen to me and understand me.
7. The other is an obstacle I must overcome.
8. Other opinions that are inconvenient are a sign of unwillingness, lack of understanding, or resistance.
9. If my attempts to salvage the situation fail, this is entirely down to others or to the situation.
10. Making mistakes is bad; I have a position and a reputation for competence to uphold.

Listed like this, they paint quite a bleak picture. But if we take into consideration that everybody has these thoughts from time to time, we can also just accept them as human nature. Whenever someone feels threatened, they will defend themselves. They will try to stay in control of the situation. It is often said that we should never go on the defensive. But that is nonsense! It is okay to go on the defensive, because to go on the defensive is human, everyone does it. The thing is to prevent yourself from getting stuck in a defensive mindset and to see the effects of a defensive mindset. Defending yourself is human, but the effects are not always desirable.

If you do not learn, you will not change your ways

Our autopilot does indeed serve a purpose. As long as we are effective and hitting our targets, there is little reason to start tweaking this highly ingenious mechanism. Especially in straightforward situations, operating in a reasonably controlled manner generally works a treat. Problems mostly arise when things get more complicated, when we have to deal with different people and different opinions, or when dealing with behavior and attitudes. In such situations with a heightened level of complexity, we soon start to produce unwanted effects.

Here are a few common examples of such unwanted effects:

- *We exchange worthless information*
  By raising the pressure and blocking out inconvenient information, people will start saying 'yes' while thinking 'no.' Or they will refrain from sharing information that we deem inconvenient, because we are not open to it.
- *We do not do as we say; this makes us unreliable*
  We often pay lip service to the (core) values of 'openness and honesty,' 'it's okay to make mistakes,' 'getting people involved,' and 'creating commitment.' But our autopilot makes us behave in a way that contradicts these values, thus making us unreliable.
- *We stimulate reactive behavior and disinterested relationships*
  The feeling that you are in control depends on the degree to which employees are calm and submissive. But you will probably claim to want proactive employees who take responsibility. You inadvertently stimulate the opposite to what you say you want to achieve.

- *We block learning*
  By shutting out input that we feel stands in the way of us achieving our goal, we are basically filtering the information we receive. This way, we make sure we only receive confirmation of our approach. But it also means we do not learn anything. And when our approach proves ineffective, our autopilot will mainly focus our attention on the situation and on others. We will therefore not learn from our own ineffectiveness either.
- *We create recurring problems*
  If we keep thinking and acting in the same way, we will also keep producing the same problems.

To recap: while we *talk* change, we *do* things that preserve the current situation. This makes that the change process is no more than a cosmetic exercise. If we do not learn, we will not change either. We can tweak structures and systems, but that will not change our way of thinking and our behavior.

The figure (inspired by Argyris) below recaps the thinking, actions, and effects of unilateral control.

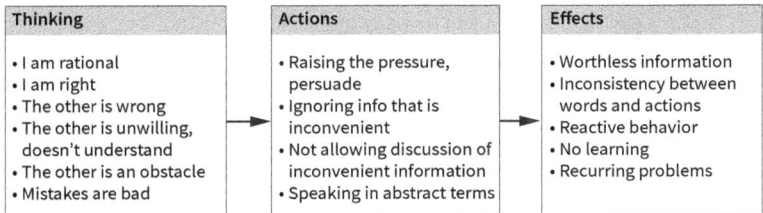

Thinking	Actions	Effects
• I am rational • I am right • The other is wrong • The other is unwilling, doesn't understand • The other is an obstacle • Mistakes are bad	• Raising the pressure, persuade • Ignoring info that is inconvenient • Not allowing discussion of inconvenient information • Speaking in abstract terms	• Worthless information • Inconsistency between words and actions • Reactive behavior • No learning • Recurring problems

Our autopilot: make sure you stay in control!

We often experience the unwanted effects as painful information, which only makes us more defensive. We will then try to sweep our ineffectiveness under the rug. And that is how the autopilot leads us into a dangerous loop: our behavior produces unwanted effects, which we subsequently try to cover up, which only leads to us producing the same effects again.

Be aware of what you do when talking about change

If you are producing (side) effects that you did not want to achieve when you started, you are not being effective. It is as simple as that. To learn means to look back on how you produced these effects. The most obvious way to do that is to look at your actions. Chances are you will find a lot of unilateral control among your actions. But what is the alternative? In the following, I will describe the kind of behavior that will help create a process of learning and change, providing real-life examples of things you could ask or say.

LEARN
Loose approach to standpoints
Earnest information sharing
Assess different paths
Real decision making
Note the effects

Loose approach to standpoints

The more you are attached to your standpoint and make it personal, the greater the chance you will go on the defensive. To learn means to accept that you rarely have the whole picture and that others may be able to help you complete the picture. This calls for a genuine interest in information that others can contribute from their perspective.

If you, as the manager, take an inflexible plan to your employees, you will probably end up putting pressure on them to accept the plan (regardless of what they really think about it). It would be much better to take the first draft of your plan to your employees, talk to them about it, and together figure out what information is still lacking.

Earnest information sharing

Be open about the information you are using and share your reasoning.

'At the last three progress reviews, it turned out that what had been agreed to had not been fulfilled (concrete information). This leads me to believe that at least some of you do not think agreements are important. And that is why I'm raising the pressure (reasoning).'

Check whether others have additional information, even when you feel the information does not help you.-

'Am I missing something? Am I rightly concerned? What is your take on the situation? Do you draw the same conclusion as I, or a different conclusion?'

Invite others to be specific, no abstractions.

A. 'This won't work here.'
B. 'Do you have any examples to back that up?' 'Do you know things about this situation that I should also know?'

Invite others to be earnest in sharing information: what does the other really think?

> 'You may say "yes" to me, but perhaps you feel pressured into saying "yes." Do you also think "yes"?'

Also give genuine information yourself.
> 'I see that you keep rejecting my ideas; this is making me less and less inclined to keep you involved; what are you trying to achieve?'

Solve the jigsaw puzzle together.

- 'I want to pick up the pace, and that's why I'm putting you under pressure. This is making you feel there is little room to exchange ideas. Therefore, you simply say 'yes', even though you are not sure this is the right path. You choose not to voice your doubts, because you don't want to make a fuss. This ultimately results in things actually taking longer. Is this an accurate assessment of how you feel about it?'
- 'Yes, and because you are not taking the time to discuss it, you are creating the impression that it doesn't really matter to you. It makes it seem as if you just want to quickly do this on the side.'
- 'That's not my intention. How can we better organize this process together?'

Assess different paths

Map out together how you can get one step ahead in the (change) process. The main thing is then to identify the expected effects of each path.

'If we were to take some time to discuss the desired change, you would feel more involved. But my concern is that it will take a long time. That would put me with my back against the wall. And that's why I keep the pressure on. What is your impression? How realistic is my concern?'

Real decision making

As soon as you have mapped out the paths, choose one based on the expected effects. Which path offers the greatest chance of success? Making a choice together, as opposed to unilaterally imposing your decision on others, will create a sense of responsibility and action.

Note the effects

Now take a look at the effects that you produce.

- 'I keep suggesting things to you because I believe they will spur you on; what effect is it having on you?' Or:
- 'I realize that I ask about progress a lot, but that's because I'm getting too little information from you all. Am I rightly concerned? What effect is my behavior having on you? How can you help me loosen the reigns more?'

There will be a learning curve to putting this into practice. But you will find that even the very first attempts will produce effects that you never produced before. You are giving others scope to feel co-responsible. Your equality-based approach will invite the other to come up with improvement initiatives.

Breakthrough 7

How effective is your behavior?

Examine how you contribute to the situation and what behavior produces better effects. And then ask yourself what behavior you think will produce better effects. Go from intervention to understanding.

The following will help you with this process of introspection.

✗ How open are you in sharing information that speaks against your idea or approach?

✗ How do you know that you are right? What information could others (employees or other co-workers) have to make the picture complete?

✗ Could others have information that proves you wrong? If so, what are you doing to get that information out in the open?

✗ How often do people say 'yes' to you and subsequently do 'no'? What are the chances of them saying 'yes' and thinking 'no'? Why do they do that in dealings with you?

✗ What can you do to shape the change you want in the here and now in the way you communicate with others?

Look at the suggestions under LEARN (page 58) and determine your strategy. How will you proceed?

Getting change unstuck by thinking differently

Sometimes, changing your behavior to get a situation unstuck is unsuccessful, such as when you find yourself unable to say the words or you keep getting the same effects. That is when you must go deeper: explore your thoughts about the situation.

If your assessment of the situation adds to the difficulty, the solution is to adopt a different perspective. A perspective that is not focused on unilateral control, but instead on learning and changing together. Okay, imagine your behavior produces unwanted effects, such as distance between you and your employees or a weakened sense of responsibility among employees. What would happen if you were to think as follows?

Ten thoughts that go with collective learning and change

1. *I am part of the difficult situation.*
2. *My impression of the situation is based on incomplete information.*
3. *My behavior leads to unwanted (side) effects.*
4. *The other is also rational and has good intentions.*
5. *The other has additional information that will help us get a better picture of the situation.*
6. *The other can contribute other information or different reasoning to trigger different insights.*
7. *If we do not listen to each other, we will only perpetuate the situation.*
8. *We all make mistakes, and we do it all the time. We can learn only if we accept that and openly explore our ineffectiveness.*

9. *Right or wrong is not interesting. It is all about exchanging valid information to identify the best direction together.*

10. *If my attempts to salvage the situation fail, I am not being effective.*

Breakthrough 8

How to get the change process unstuck by thinking differently

Look at the situation from breakthrough 6 again. Or take another situation that you thought was difficult, such as a tricky meeting with one or several of your co-workers. You felt that you were not getting anywhere, that they didn't understand you and/or didn't want to cooperate. Now look at the same situation while bearing in mind one or several of the ten thoughts that go with collective learning and change.

What effect does that have? Are you inclined to handle the situation differently? If you are, what would you do differently?

Are you managing to apply this thinking to your situation? Personally, I sometimes simply cannot even imagine that the other has good intentions. Or I am absolutely convinced I am right. But that thinking is probably precisely why situations become difficult and persistent. Changing the way we think is by no means easy. But if you pull it off, it will create a lot of space and momentum.

The following figure (based on Argyris) recaps the insights about learning and change.

Thinking	Actions	Effects
• I am part of the (difficult) situation • I know only part of the relevant information • The other also has good intentions • The other has additional information • Change requires us to openly learn from our (in)effectiveness • Mistakes are food for thought	• Taking a loose approach to standpoints • Being open about what information you are using and sharing your reasoning • Exploring additional information • Jointly examining the inconsistencies between intentions and effects • Exploring alternative behavior together	• Genuine information • Consistency between words and actions • Proactive behavior • Learning from mistakes • Revived change process

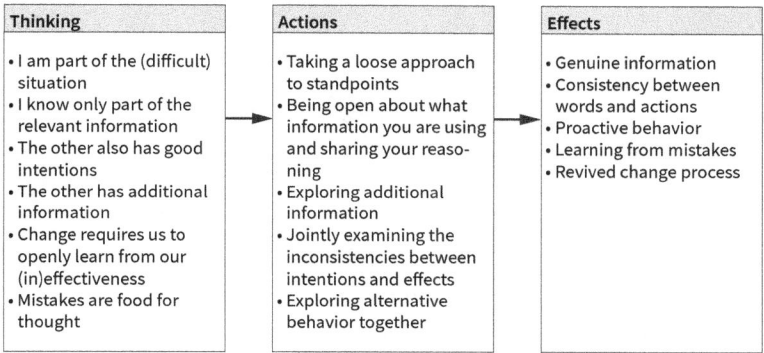

Learning and changing together: how can we create real change?

Switch to manual mode

Defensive behavior is human. When you find yourself in an uneasy, embarrassing, or threatening situation, you will automatically go on the defensive. Initially, it will be quite hard to even recognize such defensive behavior afterwards, let alone to see how it was you who deadlocked the situation.

The next step is to catch yourself doing it. The moment you feel uneasy and start to brace yourself, you know that your autopilot has been triggered. The challenge at that point is to count to ten and try to switch back to manual mode. The following phrases will help you override your autopilot.

'I'm trying hard to push my way through, but it is not getting us anywhere. I'd better quit doing that. Shall we try something else?'

'Does this help, what I'm doing now?' 'We're not making any progress, we're stagnating.' 'I don't know what to do either right now.'
'I'm trying to convince you and you keep resisting. We are not going to get anywhere like this.'

These phrases are a handy way to turn a defensive talk into another direction. After that, there are many things you can say, but one specific question is often a good one to ask: 'What am I doing that is making you respond this way?'

Breakthrough 9

How to breathe new life into the change process
Change will grind to a halt if there is no learning. Better change requires better learning. Use the insights presented in this chapter and go through the learning process on the next page.

Do not complain about the effects of your own behavior

Perhaps the way of learning and changing as described in the previous section does not sit well with you. Sometimes I get responses such as: 'We simply cannot make all decisions democratically?' and, 'Surely, they should also be able to just do what I ask them to do?' These are very legitimate responses. I want to stress that this book is about change processes relating to behavior, attitude, and working (and collaboration) methods. We are therefore not talking about implementing a new system, rules, or a procedure, but instead about things such as fanning the flame

Examine the effects
- What effect is your behavior having?
- Put this question to those who might be able to answer it. Especially when you are scared of the answer.
- Which effects did you not want?

Are you willing to change your behavior?

yes | no

Examine your behavior
- What behavior led to the unwanted effects?
- What different behavior do you expect to produce better effects?
- Put this behavior into practice at the next opportunity.

Does the new behavior produce the desired effect?

yes   no

Are you willing to change your behavior?

yes | no

Examine your thinking about the situation
- What is your thinking about yourself, the other, and the situation?
- What kind of different thinking do you expect to produce better effects?
- Try to change your perspective on the situation and adopt behavior that matches that perspective.

Does the new behavior produce the desired effect?

yes   no

of employees' entrepreneurial spirit, improving collaboration, or bridging the gap between management and employees. These are simply not things you can implement unilaterally. But you can learn together how to do things differently. And the effects might just surprise you.

Any approach will do, as long as you achieve the effects that you have set out to achieve in the way you want to achieve them. And as long as you accept possible unwanted side effects as a product of your actions, you will be consistent. But you will not be consistent if you unilaterally impose things on people and then complain about their lack of commitment. Or if you are not prepared to take criticism of your approach but still ask people to come up with ideas. Or if you invariably take the initiative and call people out on their apathetic attitude? If so, you are basically complaining about the effects of your own behavior. And that undermines your credibility.

When you see that your approach is backfiring, there are only two ways in which you can react to that without being inconsistent. Either you stick with your approach and accept the outcome, or you choose learning and try a different approach. Both are consistent. One manager once told me: 'Look, I just want to get somewhere now. So I just want them to do as I say. I understand very well that my people are apathetic and limit themselves to doing what I ask them to do. That's entirely down to me and I don't blame them for that. In fact, I even told them that. I'll figure out later how to do things differently in the future, but for now I think we need this firm approach.'
Think of it what you will, but this manager is consistent, and his credibility is probably still intact. He owns the effects of his

behavior. You could perhaps worry about what will happen 'later', but that is not an issue now.

See what you do when the going gets tough

1. *Whenever a situation becomes difficult, threatening, or uneasy, your autopilot will take over. Your autopilot will divert you away from what you claim to want. The overriding instruction: make sure you stay in control!*

2. *Without realizing it, you pile on the pressure, try to convince others, and disregard inconvenient information. You consider yourself a reasonable person and take other opinions as resistance and a lack of understanding.*

3. *This is how you, unwittingly and without realizing it, produce unwanted effects. Others will tell you 'yes' while thinking 'no,' feel disengaged and pull out. Meanwhile, you are not learning, and you are being inconsistent. In short: you are obstructing the change and learning process.*

4. *If your behavior is having unwanted effects, switch to manual mode. Examine (together) what kind of behavior and what kind of thinking about the situation are producing these effects. Effective change is to learn what behavior and/or what thinking could breathe new life into the situation.*

4 Understand how you are perpetuating the situation

Caught in a hamster wheel together

'They're not responding, so we need to be firmer.'

Director: 'How's the change process going?'

HR manager: 'We've done the first workshops. Everyone has written down an action point for themselves, so that's a good start.'

Manager 1: 'But we're going to need more than just one action point. I don't actually see them putting it into practice, to be honest.'

Manager 2: 'Yes, I worry about that as well. Just look at the departmental meeting. As always, no one contributed any items for the agenda. Not very enterprising. In the end, all the items on the agenda came from me.'

Director: 'If they don't do it themselves, you will have to take more initiative.'

By the look of it, there has not been much change. The employees still show little initiative, despite the workshops. The director orders his managers to put the screws on their direct reports. And by ordering that, he himself is basically also putting the screws on his managers. But the question is, will it help? Probably not. On the contrary, employees are likely to show even less initiative. This chapter will help you better understand how seemingly logical behavior backfires and gets you caught up in vicious cycles. It will also give you new directions on how to break the cycle.

We are perpetuating it ourselves

If you listen closely to what the managers from the example are saying, you can hear how they are perpetuating the situation themselves. Without realizing it, they are using an approach that only reinforces their employees' wait-and-see attitude. This approach, which we use all too often, is a threefold approach.

First of all, we isolate the problem as something that does not involve us. The problem these managers are seeing is that their employees are apathetic, despite the workshops and action points. Secondly, we consider ourselves as the well-thinking and initiative-taking party in the situation (the subject) and the employees as the dependent and reacting party (the object): we come up with new interventions and approaches ('we'll take the initiative') and employees undergo them.

Thirdly, we think there is a linear link between the problem and our solution: if employees are inactive, the managers will have to take the initiative...that's all, problem solved!

The elements of linear thinking

1. *Isolate the problem as something in which you are not involved.*
   ('Employees are not motivated.')
2. *Consider yourself the well-thinking and initiative-taking party and the other(s) the dependent and reacting party.*
   ('We design a workshop to motivate them.')

3. *Consider the link between the problem and your solution as a linear one.*
   ('After the workshop, the motivation problem will be solved.')

Many managers, or better still, many people consider their problems as being linear. This is logic that we understand well, and that lends itself very well for straightforward problem-solving. For example, a machine that has broken down must be repaired right away, excessive spending must be cut, and a shortage of manpower can be solved by hiring more staff. But this kind of linear thinking is pointless when applied to change processes, people and their different interests, mutual relationships, and the effectiveness of teams and individuals. In such situations, linear thinking has the opposite effect, as it confirms the behavior that is thwarting us and leads to recurring problems and self-fulfilling prophecies.

Caught in a hamster wheel

Imagine you are a manager and you feel that your employees are overly reactive and passive in their work attitude. They do not come to you with ideas to realize the required change, and they do not put your ideas into practice in the way that was agreed. You are under pressure to hit your targets, either because you have your boss breathing down your neck or because you simply do not want to look bad. So what you do is tighten the reins. You give additional instructions, you suggest a timetable, you call people to account, hoping this will lead to improvements.

Here's what this looks like:

The manager's perception

Employees   ⟶   Manager
reactive, apathetic   active, takes initiative

Very logical. Your behavior comes in response to the reactive attitude of your employees. But you do feel that even though you
push them hard, their attitude does not really seem to change. No
wonder, because these employees are doing the same thing as
you, only the other way around. They are faced with an overactive
manager who thinks he has a monopoly on showing initiative,
leading them to adopt the following attitude: 'Let's just wait and
see what the next instruction is.'

The employees' perception

Employees   ⟵   Manager
reactive, apathetic   active, takes initiative

Equally logical. The employees respond to your (overly) active
behavior and basically resign to acquiescence. And this acquiescence confirms your image of them as being passive, and so you
start to push them even harder, creating a vicious cycle.

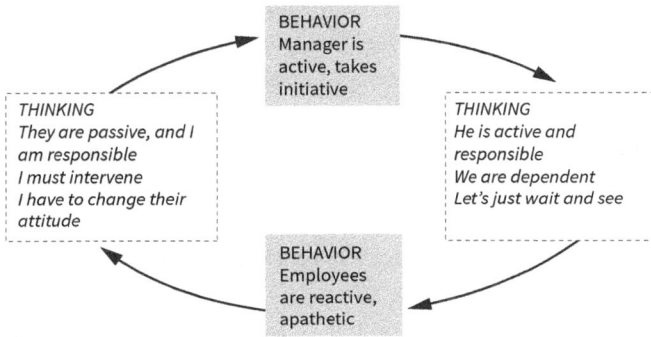

The employees see the manager's behavior, interpret it and adapt their behavior accordingly. And the manager does exactly the same. Now you can see that this is not a linear situation, but rather a so-called circular situation. It is impossible to say where the cycle starts. Manager and employees keep the cycle going together. Manager and employees are basically running after each other in a kind of hamster wheel. When one picks up the pace, the other has to keep up. And this can be quite tiring. Bill Noonan and Diana McLain Smith, both of whom were also inspired by Argyris, have described similar cycles. Diana shows how relationships between people can break down entirely as a result.

The above cycle is a common occurrence in organizations. It is perpetuated by the dominant concept of the rational manager who takes initiative and the dependent reactive employee: managers are responsible, devise interventions and approaches, and can roll these out for their dependent employees. They come up with systems and structures to structure employees' activities and they come up with ways to change employees' attitudes and behavior. This thinking can only endure if employees adopt a dependent and preferably loyal attitude. While this attitude is the effect of managers' actions, these managers see it as unwanted and try to change it through unilateral interventions, which is yet more of the same. And so they only reinforce their employees' apathy. In this kind of environment, the 'us vs. them' mentality will thrive.

Now you will also recognize the circular nature of the exchanges from the opening example.

✗ Manager 2: 'As always, no one contributed any items for the agenda. Not very enterprising. In the end, all the items for the agenda came from me.'
Where does it start? Does the manager keep putting forward items for the agenda, and have the employees simply stopped suggesting items as a result, or is it the other way around? Both assumptions are probably true.

✗ Director: 'If they won't do it of their own accord, you are going to have to take all the initiative.'
And that means that the employees will not do it of their own accord either next time...

As long as you are not aware of how the other's behavior is down to your behavior, it will never change, and you will keep running around in circles in your hamster wheel. Take a look at the following statements. Can you see how these are self-perpetuating?

• 'People are always late for a meeting, I can never start on time.'
• 'They are rather passive, so I have to take the initiative quite forcefully.'
• 'My employees aren't doing it themselves, so that's why I'm inviting you now.'
• 'Employees will probably resist; I have to tighten the reins.'

- 'Employees oppose the management, they have an "us vs. them" mentality.'

The concept of the rational and responsible manager and the dependent employee is very much a product of the zeitgeist. In an age where it was normal and preferred that employees did exactly what their boss told them to do, this concept worked fine. But in an age where management is all about stimulating entrepreneurial spirit, personal responsibility, and empowerment, the concept ceases to be effective: the manager claims to value independence and an enterprising attitude, but still (without realizing it) breeds dependence and apathy through his behavior.

What you think is what you see is what you get

The above statements are based on assumptions and convictions about each other, about the other. We think we know what others are like, how they think, and how they behave. Generally, we fail to check whether our assumptions and convictions are accurate. Quite the opposite, they drive our perceptions without us realizing it. And when things have ground to a halt, these convictions are mostly unfavorable: the other is unwilling, the other cannot be trusted, the other does not want to adapt, the other is unable to reflect, the other only sees the negative in managers...

Our preconceptions of the other make us selective in what we see. Any behavior and statements that do not fit our preconceived picture, we simply choose not to see. This is how we keep our world manageable. As long as we take these convictions as truth and do not discuss them, they are the fuel that keeps the hamster wheel turning.

Take the example of the manager of the organization where the working atmosphere had turned sour. Trust between management and employees had dropped to an unprecedented low. The manager said that his employees lacked the ability to reflect and could therefore not engage in an open discussion about their role. Prompted by this conviction and the threat he felt, he subsequently allowed his autopilot to kick in: he disengaged and imposed compulsory instructions on his staff. Employees saw a withdrawn manager who dumped top-down instructions on them. Some submissively executed the instructions, others resisted. But they all had their impression that the manager was not taking them seriously confirmed. None of them looked at their own behavior. And this, in turn, confirmed the manager's impression that the employees are unable to reflect and simply oppose the management. This ultimately created a self-fulfilling prophecy. The manager's preconceptions drove his behavior and the effect of the behavior confirmed his preconceptions.

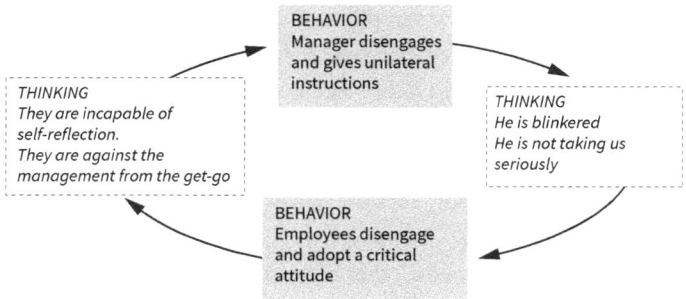

How can you tell whether you are dealing with a linear or a circular problem? You will figure that out in no time. Common signs of a circular problem:

- 'Logical interventions' do not produce logical outcomes.
- You are putting a lot of energy into it and the unwanted effects are not waning (and perhaps even growing).
- You feel knotted up inside.
- The same problem keeps coming back.
- You feel you are going around in circles.

When that happens, you can safely assume that you are indeed going around in circles. In most other cases, you will be facing a linear problem-->solution situation. That is when you should keep things simple and just implement the solution.

Breakthrough 10

What hamster wheel are you caught up in?

You are not getting anywhere together. You feel like you're going around in circles. This is probably not merely a feeling. It is likely that you are indeed caught in a hamster wheel, together with the others (your employees?). The following questions will help you become aware of your unchecked convictions, their impact on your behavior, and the consequences for the other.

✗ What convictions do you have about the other? Consider things such as their level of motivation, autonomy, willingness, problem-solving ability.

✗ What have you seen that makes you hang on to these convictions?

✗ Be aware of the fact that as long as you do not openly discuss these convictions, they will drive your perception. Are there perhaps any examples that show that your impression is not entirely accurate?

✗   What effects are your convictions having on your behavior towards the other?

✗   How do you think the other interprets your behavior? What convictions might he or she have about you? And how are you confirming those convictions through your behavior?

✗   What effects are their convictions having on their behavior? To what degree does that match the impression you already had of them?

Now try to fill in the blanks in the cycle on the next page. You will find it easier if you stick to the order below.

1.   What behavior by the other(s) bothers you and would you want to change?

2.   What are your thoughts/convictions about the situation?

3.   What behavior do you display?

4.   What thoughts/convictions could the other(s) have about the situation?

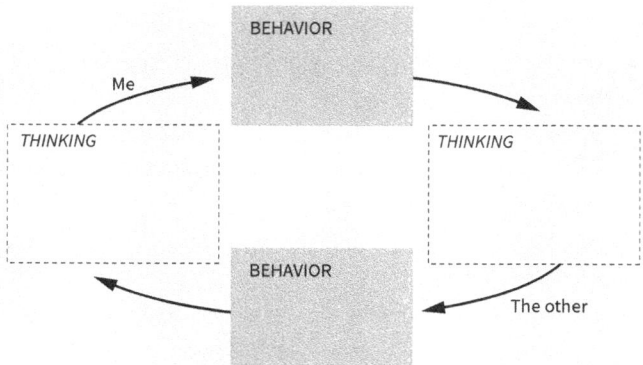

Let's do away with resistance

'Resistance' is the single most commonly used term in the context of change processes. We have grown used to employees resisting our change initiatives. And we fully expect to have to design strategies to break down their resistance. However, these convictions can easily drive us into a circular process.

Imagine you have a meeting scheduled later where you want to bring up an idea you have. You expect resistance. What kind of behavior are you likely to display in this situation? You will probably be apprehensive (and perhaps not feel very secure), use well-prepared arguments to increase the pressure on people and to defend your idea. In short, you activate your autopilot and try to stay in control of the situation. What effect do you suppose this behavior will have? Precisely what you feared going into the meeting: resistance! People will be on guard, oppose your idea, or disengage. You will think: see, I knew this would happen. And then you dial up the pressure.

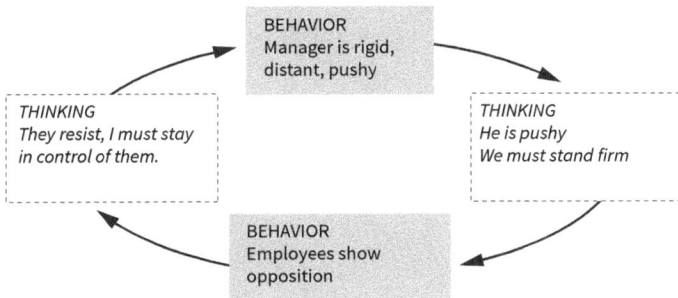

BEHAVIOR
Manager is rigid, distant, pushy

THINKING
They resist, I must stay in control of them.

THINKING
He is pushy
We must stand firm

BEHAVIOR
Employees show opposition

Resistance as a self-fulfilling prophecy. This turns out to be a persistent pattern in practice. Since we experience this kind of situation as challenging, we switch to autopilot, which makes us label as resistance any ideas that are not aligned with our own, making the situation even more challenging and our urge to stay in control even stronger. I am not saying that all resistance from others is something we create ourselves, but I am saying that our behavior often adds to it.

The concept of resistance is not helpful in this context. In fact, it is often inconsistent to label certain behavior as resistance. Many organizations pay great lip service to their pursuit of 'open and honest' interactions. What could be more open and honest than people not being afraid to be critical of your approach or suggest a different point of view? If we were consistent with our claimed core values, we should be rewarding that. But our behavior does not work that way. Whenever open and honest information does not suit us, we activate the previously mentioned cycle. So even though we claim to want 'openness and honesty', we struggle to put it into practice. It is far easier for us to deal with people who say 'yes' and think 'no'. Not open and honest at all...

Breakthrough 11

How are you fueling the resistance?

You experience resistance on your team. You try to stay in charge and prepare team meetings well. You've got another team meeting coming up soon. But you already feel all knotted up inside just thinking about it. It is bound to be another difficult meeting.

Try changing the way you prepare for the meeting. Do not try to come up with ways to intervene, but instead try to understand the situation. The following questions will help you with that.

✗   Why are you expecting resistance?

✗   What past examples are you basing this on?

✗   What was others' and your behavior like in these cases?

✗   What effects are your preconceptions ('they will resist') having on your behavior?

✗   And what effect is your behavior having on them?

✗   Why would they behave in that way? What positive intention could be hidden behind that?

✗   What information might they have that you don't have yet? How could that improve your idea?

✗   How could you engage with others to achieve shared understanding instead of unilateral intervention?

In the remainder of this book, I will not use the term resistance. As far as I am concerned, the concept of resistance can be consigned to the wastebasket.

My boss doesn't inspire me

Another example of a hamster wheel: how do I inspire my employees? This is a question that often pops up in discussions about leadership. Managers try hard to inspire and motivate their people but are often unsuccessful. What would you think about the following vicious cycle?

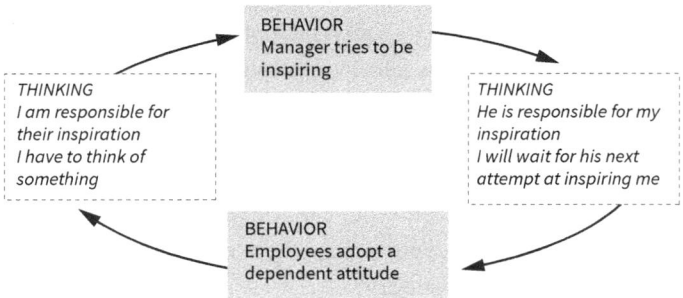

THINKING
I am responsible for
their inspiration
I have to think of
something

BEHAVIOR
Manager tries to be
inspiring

THINKING
He is responsible for my
inspiration
I will wait for his next
attempt at inspiring me

BEHAVIOR
Employees adopt a
dependent attitude

If you, as a manager, worry about how to inspire your people, you are reinforcing the concept of the manager as the rational and initiative-taking party and of employees as the dependent and reactive party, which makes you responsible for their inspiration. And your attempts to inspire them often only lead your employees to feel that you, as their boss, are indeed responsible for inspiring them. This always backfires.

I often hear employees complain that their manager does not inspire them. They are basically making someone else responsible for their inspiration. It is time to wake up. You are maintaining this status quo together. What happened to the idea that everyone is responsible for their own inspiration? You should focus on your own inspiration as a manager: how do you feel about your profession, about your job, about your life? Are you inspired yourself? If you are not, you will not succeed in inspiring others either. If you are inspired, and talk about your profession with passion, chances are that others will follow.

You cannot break out of the cycle on your own

Just imagine. You are fresh out of a meeting and realize that you did most of the talking, while others were overly quiet. You asked them for their opinion on various occasions but got little to no reply. During the actual meeting, you were right in the middle of it and not aware of the vicious cycle you were all caught up in. After all, your autopilot was in control.

Now, looking back on the meeting, you realize that your respective behaviors are mutually reinforcing. What now? How do you break out of this cycle?

My research has shown that this awareness tends to make managers step back and think about how to act next time. They tell themselves to be more passive next time and ask more questions. And at the next meeting, they put all these good intentions into practice. But then they face a surprise. The resulting situation could be like the following.

> Manager: 'How do you think we should handle this?'
> Silence.
> Manager: 'Any ideas?'
> Silence.
> Employee: 'What do you think?'
> Manager: 'I'd really like to get your input on this.'
> Silence.
> Manager (uncomfortable): 'You could, for example, think about...'

What exactly is happening here? The manager has unilaterally decided to step out of the hamster wheel by changing his behavior. His employees, however, are completely in the dark as to his reasoning behind this and they are still running in the hamster wheel. They will likely think to themselves 'why is he suddenly asking questions, he never used to before?' It will not take them long to make the manager revert to his old behavior, pull him back into the hamster wheel. The manager has tried and will relapse into his old trusted pattern. This pattern, which was built over time by managers and employees together, protects itself.

This is a great example that shows that simply changing our behavior will not save the situation. The fact of the matter is that the manager's approach is basically the product of the same thinking that created the cycle in the first place: I am the manager and therefore the rational and initiative-taking party here and you employees are the dependent and reactive party. When I see that communication between us is stalling, I unilaterally decide to change tack, without sharing my reasoning with you. And thus, the manager, despite his best intentions, still pushes the employees into a position of dependency.

Stopping the hamster wheel

Real change is something you achieve together. If you realize that you are all caught in a vicious cycle together, you should openly engage about it with those involved. Learning together will then soon turn into a shared understanding of how you are indeed blocking (change) processes, and subsequently into a joint effort to explore alternative ways. This is how you take each other seriously as responsible and well-thinking people, and how you basically break the cycle right away.

Breakthrough 12

How to break out of recurring patterns

Okay, so you realize that you are all caught up in a hamster wheel together. Perhaps you have even already discussed the situation with (like-minded) people who are not directly involved. Understandable, but that will not help you much.

Break out of the cycle by discussing it with the people involved.

1. Openly discuss the vicious cycle and stress that you yourself are also instrumental in keeping it going. Let the others know that you assume that everyone only has the best of intentions in the situation, but that you all unwittingly have each other in a hold.
2. Ask whether they recognize what you are saying. Do they see the same pattern? How do they experience the situation?
3. Explain that you want to break out of the pattern by changing your behavior and approach. Ask them whether they acknowledge their role in the situation.
4. Discuss what individual behavior your people think could break the pattern.
5. Agree on how to maintain open communication about the follow-up.

You can bring up the vicious cycle by presenting your view on it, but also by asking questions and thus mapping out the situation together. Here are a few examples.

- 'I think we're going wrong somewhere. I've seen that you are often rather standoffish in meetings. I do most of the talking and I am the one coming up with ideas. I think this may be making you more reluctant to engage. Is this an accurate assessment?'
- 'I've noticed that you are taking a wait-and-see approach. Am I doing something that keeps you from voicing your opinion? If I am, what is it?'
- 'I've figured out that I tend to become more reserved when I experience a situation as challenging. As a result, I lose touch with you, causing you to distance yourself from me as well. And this, in turn, makes the situation even more challenging for me. Is this something you recognize?'

After reaching shared awareness of how you are perpetuating the situation, the next step is to explore alternative ways. Here are a few options.

- 'How can we take a more effective approach to such change processes?'
- 'I don't want to give my opinion so quickly, I primarily want to give you space to give yours. Would that help? That would require you to try to actively give your opinion.'
- 'How could you help me better stay engaged, also when things are challenging for me?'

The good thing about vicious cycles is that there is no culprit who started it. You are keeping it going together. And so there is less embarrassment involved in recognizing and owning up to your role in perpetuating the cycle. This is a low-threshold way of making difficult processes a subject of discussion.

Leaders launch the learning process

In all examples, the manager is the one taking the initiative to talk about the situation. Needless to say, employees could also take the initiative. After all, they are equally involved in keeping the vicious cycle going. More so than managers, employees need courage to bring the situation up for discussion. Because as an employee, you are at the mercy of your manager's response. Other than that, the mechanism of broaching the subject is the same. You could start off by saying:

> 'I feel that we have each other in a hold. I am very on guard and feel reluctant, because I think you are not giving me enough space. And perhaps you are keeping me on a tight leash precisely because of my reluctant attitude. Is this something you recognize?'

In practice, many employees sense a kind of threshold that keeps them from drawing their manager's attention to difficult situations. Again, this basically confirms the pattern of the active manager and the dependent employee. And if we then say that it is up to the manager to initiate new dynamics, we are yet again confirming this pattern: 'Let my manager set the tone first; he is responsible.' Still, what has turned out far more effective in real life is for the manager to first reflect on how he contributes to making the situation what it is.

Understand how you are perpetuating the situation
1. *If you feel you are going around in circles, you probably are. Your behavior reinforces the unwanted behavior of the other, which in turn provokes your behavior. That is how vicious*

cycles and self-fulfilling prophecies are born. You are all running after each other in a hamster wheel.

2. *Your preconceptions of the other make you selective in what you see. This is how you keep creating your own confirmation. As long as you fail to validate your preconceptions, they are the fuel that drives the hamster wheel.*

3. *If you expect your employees to resist, you will automatically adopt a firmer and more authoritarian attitude and yield precisely the resistance you were afraid of. This is resistance as a self-fulfilling prophecy.*

4. *Vicious cycles have a self-protection mechanism: when you decide to step out of the cycle, the others will soon draw you back in.*

5. *To stop the hamster wheel, you need to learn together: how are we keeping each other trapped in this situation; how could we do things differently?*

5

Dare to discuss the undiscussable

How we laugh our way out of real change

'Let's not make it sound worse than it is.'

> Director (in a management team meeting): 'We're discussing the progress of our development program. You were all supposed to engage with your respective teams about employees' sense of security. Let's see what you all found out.'
>
> Manager 1: 'I don't think there are any problems at my department. We are a small team and the atmosphere is good.'
>
> Manager 2: 'I want to be open with you. This week, two of your team members came to me. Both said that they feel uneasy around you. Perhaps there is more than you know.'
>
> All MT members remain silent...
>
> Manager 2: 'It seems that you say things to them that undermine their sense of security.'
>
> More silence....
>
> Director: 'Well, don't we all say things sometimes that turn out to be ill-advised in hindsight? Let's not make a big deal out of this, let's continue.'

This is an awkward, perhaps even painful, situation: your employees complain about you to one of your peers. It is very hard to come out of this situation with your dignity intact. Thankfully, the director intervenes. He plays down the situation and gives the manager a way out. Or perhaps not thankfully? The issue has been raised and is out there, but it has been quashed and is not open to discussion. The management team has stayed in control, but there was no learning. And learning was precisely what they set out to do. Was this the autopilot at work? This chapter will show how we deploy sophisticated strategies to sweep aside inconvenient information and consequently fail to learn. The question is how to foster learning and change.

An inconvenient truth

To achieve effective change, we need to be willing to learn. And to learn, we need to be aware of our (in)effectiveness. If our behavior does not produce the desired effects, we must change our behavior. It seems so simple. On paper. But in real life, it turns out to be far from simple. This is due to our tendency not to address honest information about our ineffectiveness. We try to protect ourselves and others from the awkward situation that would arise if we were to openly talk about this. Or, in other words, we go on the defensive.

Let's say you are a manager who, in a meeting, is piling pressure on employees to get them to accept an idea of yours. Employees ultimately say yes to be done with it. You wanted genuine commitment, but you got fake commitment. Basically, you are being ineffective and have sown the seeds of a plastic change process. The employees know that and so do you, or at least you have a gut feeling about it. What is keeping you from openly discussing this honest information about your ineffectiveness? Employees could say:

'Because of the pressure you put on me, I'm inclined to say "yes", while I really think "no". Is that what you want?'

This would be very valuable information. It would make it real. But employees will not quickly come out with these kinds of comments. And as a manager you could say:

'I feel I'm piling on the pressure. You tell me "yes", but I wonder whether you really mean it.'

Again, this is something that we will not easily say. After all, you never know what response you might get. One of my inspirations, Chris Argyris, conducted extensive research into defensive behavior. He discovered that whenever we try to cover up inconvenient information, we also cover up this behavior in the process. This is because if we would not cover it up, we could get strange statements such as:

'I think we'd better keep this subject under wraps, because it's rather painful for me,' or: 'You asked for my opinion; I can tell you the truth or make you feel good about yourself, which one do you choose?'

Given that the defensive behavior obstructs our learning, it also obstructs effective change. It leads to conservation of the current situation and with that to recurring problems. If you develop a kind of sensitivity to it, you will be able to recognize defensive behavior. First in others, and ultimately also in yourself.

Defensive strategies: blocking your own change

I have discovered that we use highly sophisticated ways to brush inconvenient information aside and never get it out in the open for discussion: defensive strategies. It is a kind of behavior that seems entirely normal at first, but which is, in essence, intended to prevent painful information from surfacing and inconvenient situations from occurring. These behaviors are widely accepted in board rooms, on management teams, and among managers in dealings with employees.

Here's an example. Imagine employees pretend to commit, because telling you 'no' is not a realistic option. They undergo the process without really feeling responsible for it (*the commit strategy*). The manager will then sense that the employees are not really committed, but he will choose to ignore that because bringing it up will probably lead to an awkward situation (*the ignore strategy*). If the manager were to cotton on to the lack of active commitment, he would find himself in a tricky situation: he can choose to find out why employees do not really engage, but it is safer to not ask any questions, to reason that everything will work out fine (*the downplay strategy*) or to simply deny the problem and increase the pressure (*the denial strategy*). Meanwhile, the manager considers the employees responsible for the problems and the employees believe the problems are caused by the manager or circumstances (*the pass-the-buck strategy*). Managers and employees develop increasingly resolute and not very positive thoughts about each other they do, however, not share these with each other but instead with like-minded people (*the withdrawal strategy*). Employees find someone to talk to about the manager who won't listen. The manager, in turn, uses management team meetings to complain about employees' lack of commitment. In management team meetings, the attending managers generally avoid making things difficult for each other. The moment the situation threatens to take a compromising turn, someone will crack a joke and change the subject (*the humor strategy*), play down the problem (*the downplay strategy*) and the managers will not call each other to account: if you don't call me to account, I won't call you to account either (*the non-intervention strategy*).

Recognize this? Perhaps you have seen others do it. These defensive strategies work remarkably well and are difficult to spot. They help us in talking about change approaches and use our behavior to protect the current situation. Because we are not learning...

The following is an anthology of the various defensive strategies that I have observed in my research. When a situation becomes compromising, you will soon see one or several of these strategies pop up.

Defensive strategies

✗ The commit strategy: when your boss pushes you to commit, just say that you're committed, even if you're not ('Okay, I'm in').

✗ The ignore strategy: when confronted with things that you find difficult to deal with, such as the fact that your employees are not really committed, don't try to figure out why; instead, increase the pressure ('let's stick to our agreements').

✗ The denial strategy: when a situation becomes threatening or awkward, deny the problem ('there are no problems at my department').

✗ The withdrawal strategy: in cases of a communication breakdown, don't openly address it with everyone involved; instead, withdraw and design your next intervention or discuss the situation with like-minded people ('how can I break their resistance?').

✗ The pass-the-buck strategy: when your approach/behavior proves ineffective, blame it on the circumstances and/or on others ('employees just don't want to change' or 'managers just don't want to listen to us').

✗ The downplay strategy: when the situation has become threatening or awkward, play down the problem to reduce it to manageable proportions ('let's not make a big deal out of this').

✗ The we strategy: keep the conversation impersonal by speaking in terms of 'our responsibility' and what 'we should do' ('we should focus more on these problems').

✗ The evasion strategy: when things get too personal, change the subject to the others or to general observations, such as employees, middle management, or the company as a whole ('we lack a unifying organizational culture').

✗ The non-intervention strategy: do not address someone else's ineffectiveness, so that they won't address yours either ('I know he's very busy, so I can't blame him for not sticking to the agreement').

✗ The humor strategy: when the situation has become threatening or awkward, crack a joke and change the subject ('you can't help it, you're a northerner after all...').

Looking at these defensive strategies like this, at a glance, they come across as disingenuous and malicious. The truth is, however, that we all do it without considering ourselves to be disingenuous and malicious. It is apparently human nature and subconscious behavior. It helps us stay in control of a situation in the short term. But it also stands in the way of our learning and change in the long term.

Please note: the defensive strategies listed above are expressly not to be considered manifestations of resistance to change. These are, instead, forms of behavior that we resort to subconsciously and that even undermine the change we are claiming to pursue. It is not that we oppose change, but rather that we are afraid of inconvenient (learning) situations.

If you look closely, you can see that some strategies emerge mainly in the relationship between manager and employees (the commit, ignore, denial, and withdrawal strategies), while others are triggered mainly between equals on teams (the we, evasion, non-intervention, humor strategies). And the remaining strategies are used in both kinds of relationships (the pass-the-buck and the downplay strategies).

You might now think: but isn't humor potentially very helpful in keeping things light and doesn't playing things down help keep them manageable? And you would be right in thinking that. The effect of such behavior cannot be judged without looking at the situation. Humor is great. But jokes do not help when they are used to cut off a discussion that deals with valuable information.

Breakthrough 13

How to recognize defensive strategies

If you want to do more than just talk about change, and want to really learn and change, it would help a great deal if you were able to recognize both your own and others' defensive strategies. Mind you, this is by no means easy to do, as the behavior that goes with these strategies comes across as entirely logical and innocent. To be able to identify the strategies, you are going to have to fine-tune your feelers, which is a matter of practicing a lot. You can keep it light by taking a playful approach. Copy or photocopy the following list (or the defensive strategies scorecard in the appendices) and play the game.

Bingo!

Situation: a team talk about a non-straightforward subject, such as the progress of the change process, team effectiveness, or the level of effort put in by individual team members.

Gameplay: all team members receive the below checklist with defensive strategies that people often use in team situations. As soon as you hear a defensive strategy you recognize, find it on the list and check the box. As soon as a team member has checked three boxes, he or she shouts 'bingo!' The game is then paused to allow this team member to present his or her observations.

❑ The pass-the-buck strategy

Whenever your approach/behavior turns out to be ineffective, blame it on circumstances and/or someone else.

- ❏ The downplay strategy
  Whenever a situation becomes threatening or awkward, downplay the problem to make it manageable again.
- ❏ The we strategy
  Keep the conversation impersonal by speaking in terms of 'our responsibility' and 'what we must do.'
- ❏ The evasion strategy
  When a discussion comes too close to home, change the subject to other people or general observations, such as employees, middle management, or the company.
- ❏ The non-intervention strategy
  Don't mention the ineffectiveness of others, so they won't mention yours either.
- ❏ The humor strategy
  When a situation becomes threatening or awkward, crack a joke and change the subject.

Defensive strategies are a form of self-protection

By telling you about defensive behavior, I am putting you in a catch-22. This is because as long as you are not aware of your defensive behavior, you can carry on indefinitely. There will be less learning for you and your colleagues, and real change will be stifled, but you have nothing to be ashamed of. If, on the other hand, you become aware of your defensive behavior, you instantly face the question of whether or not to talk about it. If you do not, chances are you will feel less responsible for the success of the process, simply because you are distancing yourself from it. If you do decide to openly talk about it, you might end up causing problems. What is clever about these strategies is that they are intended to prevent awkward situations. So, if you create an awkward situation by exposing defensive strategies, you will probably bear the brunt of it.

Here's an example. During a management team meeting I sat in on, I noticed that the team members were very good at deploying the humor strategy and the downplay strategy. I shared my observation with the director and head of HR.

> Me: 'At the meeting the other day, I noticed that you tend to go out of your way to not have to talk about difficult issues. You use some very effective strategies for that: the humor strategy and the downplay strategy. When things get challenging or personal, there's always someone who either cracks a quick joke and distracts the attention or says that the issue should not be blown out of proportion.'
> Head of HR to the director (laughingly): 'That means YOU can't make jokes about southerners anymore.'
> They both laugh.
> Me: 'Thank you! This is exactly what I mean by the humor strategy. As you can see, it works extremely well.'
> Director: 'Come on, you're exaggerating quite a bit here...'

Both strategies turned out to be very effective. When you, as a team member, want to bring these kinds of strategies up for discussion, you are going to have to be very sure of yourself and stand firm. You will find this easier after you have addressed the issue of defensive behavior together and how it affects (team) effectiveness. That gives you a foothold.

Discussing the undiscussable

My research has shown that bringing defensive strategies up for discussion almost always ends up triggering them in the short term. But in the long term, it will reduce defensive behavior in the team. You could say there is a delayed effect. If you manage to stick with it, to keep the focus on these strategies, they will be weakened. By flagging these strategies every time they are used, they will slowly but surely lose strength. If, for example, it has happened five times on your team that people try to play down things such as your ineffectiveness in the change process or put the blame on someone else, and you made the team stop and think about this defensive tendency each time, chances are the sixth time they will think: 'we're doing it again' and 'what are we doing?'

Making defensive behavior a topic for open discussion requires skill. It is something you can learn by sticking to a few basic principles.

1. *Discuss the behavior you observe and its effects*
   The below chart will give you something to go by. Giving feedback on someone's intentions leads to anger and is pointless: you give feedback about something you know nothing about and the other knows everything about. For example: 'you are trying to thwart progress' or: 'you don't want to change your behavior at all.' Feedback on behavior works better but does not quite go far enough.

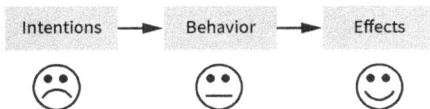

For example: 'when push comes to shove, you play down the problem...' The most effective tactic is to discuss both behavior and the effect. You would then add: '… and the effect of that is that we are not learning and not getting anywhere.' Feedback on the effects is a way to give the other information of which he/she is probably not aware. Now that is truly helpful information! You can end by asking the other about their intentions. As in: 'this is what I have observed and that is the effect, but what was your intention?'

2. *Be neutral in identifying inconsistency*

Value judgments are counterproductive. Good and wrong are often subjective and offer no learning opportunity. The art is to get the other (and yourself) to act consistently. For example: 'what you want (a safe working atmosphere) is not consistent with what you do (block discussion of open and honest feedback).' You can keep displaying the same behavior and accept that the working atmosphere is not as safe as you would like it to be or you can change your behavior and help create an open and safe working atmosphere. Both options are consistent.

It is my experience that talking about defensive strategies becomes easier with some practice: the more you do it, the easier it gets. This is illustrated nicely by the following lines I have heard at management team meetings:

- 'Let's not talk about others, but let's start by looking at our own role' (in response to the evasion strategy).
- 'Gentlemen, we are changing the subject with jokes' (in response to the humor strategy).

- 'Wait a minute. Now the pressure is on, the problem suddenly doesn't seem so big. Is that correct?' (in response to the downplay strategy).

Breakthrough 14
How to talk about your team's (in)effectiveness

To learn is to examine our (in)effectiveness. Once we are able to recognize and acknowledge that we resort to certain defensive behavior, the challenge is to openly talk about what that does for us and what it costs us. Without judging.

Imagine you and your team members arrive at the conclusion that the working climate at your company needs changing: collaboration, result-driven attitudes, communication, and/or a sense of security are all things that need to be addressed.

Instead of looking at things from a distance, get up close to it for a change. How is your team doing on this improvement target? Abide by the following two basic principles:

1. Discuss the behavior you observe and its effects.
2. Be neutral in identifying inconsistency.

Bear in mind what Peter Senge said about defensive behavior: to stay effective, defensive habits need to remain unspoken. Teams will only get caught up in these habits when they claim that they are not defensive, that everything is just fine and that everyone can say 'whatever they want'...

Dare to discuss the undiscussable

1.   As we tend to experience information about our ineffectiveness
     as inconvenient, it makes us go on the defensive. This subse-
     quently sees us try - often without realizing it - to quash any
     kind of discussion of it.
2.   We use sophisticated ways to keep painful information under
     the rug: defensive strategies. Examples include the downplay
     strategy, the ignore strategy, and the humor strategy.
3.   If you do decide to talk about these strategies, you will initially
     only activate them more. After all, they are intended to help
     you avert inconvenient situations. Once you have highlighted
     defensive behavior on various occasions, it will gradually
     weaken, giving way to learning and change.
4.   Talking and getting others to talk about these defensive habits
     requires skill. Try not to judge but identify inconsistencies neu-
     trally: this is what we want, but this is what we are doing.

6 Start small

Changing in the here and now

'Might we actually be causing this behavior?'

> HR manager: 'Many companies have core values that describe their desired culture. Ours could be: entrepreneurship, result-driven attitude, and personal responsibility.'
>
> Manager 1: 'What do you mean by insufficient entrepreneurial spirit?'
>
> HR manager: 'I mean that people tend to be passive, don't show initiative. We have all seen that, right?'
>
> Manager 1: 'Yes. But should we not ask ourselves why our people adopt a passive attitude? Could it be that we are actually encouraging that behavior in some way?'
>
> Director: 'How?'
>
> Manager 1: 'That's the puzzle we have to solve. But if we now come up with all kinds of measures to change their behavior, I doubt that we will make them less passive. In fact, I think we would be making them more passive: we take the initiative, they wait and see whatever we come up with.'

These exchanges differ enormously from the previous ones. There are no abstract concepts such as entrepreneurship, but concrete and recognizable behavior. They do not talk about what they must do differently, but about how they are perpetuating the situation. They do not suggest top-down plans but focus on their own behavior. They do not fall back on change management, but target learning and change. This way of thinking and talking is very different from what we are generally used to seeing. This chapter will show you how to get started with it.

Real change does not require change management

If you want to create a climate of change and learning, the major pitfall is that you might try to implement it using widely known change management insights and tactics. With change management, however, you will only achieve the exact opposite.

'Change management' is a concept that we should really get rid of. Because if there is one thing you cannot manage, it is real change. Sure, the implementation of soulless structures and systems you can manage. But if you take the same approach to getting people to up their game, try to innovate, feel responsible, and show initiative, you will be disappointed. You will only end up creating a soulless organization, expelling the ghost from the machine. 'Management' is all about controlling what already exists and eliminating irregularities as much as possible. However, as should be clear by now, this happens to be precisely the kind of approach that will kill change and learning.

Following on from this, the question that emerges is how to get started with creating a climate of learning and change. The following suggestions will give you a foothold from which you can get started.

Start small

Large and lengthy processes soon feel like top-down plan implementation. Instead, try to start small. When you are having a
team meeting and you know that things may get challenging or
awkward, try to catch yourself adopting defensive behavior.

Evaluate critical incidents

After a tense meeting, look back on it and reflect on your role.
Are you happy with the outcome? How effective do you think
your approach was? Did you perhaps operate on autopilot at any
point? Did you and your team end up in any vicious cycles? If you
force yourself to answer these questions, and answer them hon-
estly, you might try a different approach next time. The more
often you evaluate, the greater the chance of you catching yourself
out and realizing that you are causing the deadlock.

Talk about what you see

Instead of keeping your observations to yourself, share them with
others. This is the way forward when pursuing shared learning
and change. Try to identify together what you see and hear, without judging. Be sure to go into the inconsistency between your
ambitions and your actions.

Be open about your own role

As soon as you have become aware of how your behavior
obstructs the change process, do not hesitate to talk about this
with others. You will probably initially feel apprehensive or tense
doing it, but that is your defenses trying to take over: you want to

protect yourself. This is understandable and natural, but also part of the problem. Can you handle it?

Also help others talk about things

If you are able to show others how you are undermining the learning and change together, they will sooner start to talk about this as well. Ask them what they are seeing and invite them to flag inconsistency between what you all say and what you all do.

Take a workshop together

The way of looking and thinking formulated in this book differs greatly from our automatic and conditioned behavior. You could consider taking a workshop to shake things up. Make sure you do this together, so that you develop a shared language.

Invite an objective observer

If you are right in the middle of it, it will sometimes be difficult to assume a helicopter view to look at the process in the here and now. Ask an outsider to sit in on challenging meetings. A trained outsider will often be better at spotting inconsistencies and asking the kinds of questions that will trigger self-analysis.

Appoint someone as the team's conscience

You could appoint a team member to act as the team's conscience. This person will then find it easier to bring sensitive matters up for discussion. And if you have team members take turns being the team's conscience, it also becomes a great training exercise.

Evaluate meetings together

Evaluating together equals learning together and will (therefore) lead to change. Evaluating together allows you to step back from what you said and did in the meeting. Discuss to what degree you ended up in vicious cycles together, used defensive strategies, and generated unwanted effects.

Slow down!

To keep a clear view of what is going on, slow down. This requires patience. As soon as you realize how you might be blocking the change process and start to explore alternative ways, you will recoup that time.

Remember that all these suggestions do not apply to more straightforward matters. But as soon as you notice that things are getting difficult, that they are challenging and will cost a lot of energy, it is time to change tack. And that is where these suggestions come in, which have already more than proven themselves in real-life settings.

Change differently, talk differently

My experience is that it can be quite difficult to find the right words in trying to do your bit in creating a climate of change and learning. Before you know it, you relapse into your autopilot with widely accepted language such as 'we have to,' 'this is how it is,' 'believe me,' 'surely you understand,' 'you cannot be serious,' 'we cannot afford to,' etc. These are all turns of phrase that are intended to ensure that you stay in control of the situation, avoid hassle, and keep your footing. But you are also blocking progress, killing creativity, and undermining change and innovation.

In the previous chapters, I illustrated new insights using real-life exchanges. In the following you will find another few illustrations of conversations that seek to establish shared learning and change.

Introducing a change theme

Manager: 'But to be able to survive in the long term, we have to keep innovating. We have to keep surprising our customers.'
Employee: 'I actually think we do not need to surprise our customers. They like us because they get exactly what they want. Without fuss and smooth talking.'
Manager: 'We both want to provide the best service to customers. But we differ on the how. Let's compare the information we have about customer expectations and see whether we can come to a complete picture.'

Openly discuss dilemmas

Manager to employee: 'I have doubts. I want to give you the chance to complete this project on your own. But I'm not sure, because you are not giving me any signs of what you are doing. This makes me inclined to check up on you, which you don't like. How can we do this in a way that is good for both of us?'

Talk about change process stagnation

Manager: 'I want you all to actively commit to this policy and that's why I keep raising the pressure; but it seems to me that all this pressure is not actually making you more active. This frustrates me and makes me push you even harder. What effect is my behavior having on you?'

Employee: 'It is making us feel even less responsible.'

Manager: 'Is there a way I can support your sense of responsibility for this policy?'

Employee: 'That would require a drastic change of approach, because at the moment we do not feel taken seriously.'

Manager: 'That's not my intention, of course. What do you think I should be doing?'

Discussing progress as a management team

Manager 1: 'It's just nothing but struggle with these people. They oppose the management team a priori, and always think in terms of us vs. them.'

Manager 2: 'I can join in on the complaining, but that won't get you anywhere. What strikes me is that you also speak in terms of us vs. them, and it sounds like you oppose them a priori as well. Is that what you want?'

Manager 1: 'No...'

Manager 2: 'If that is your thinking, it might just impact on how you behave towards them. What kind of manager are they getting?'

You can see that there are a few recurring aspects: taking a situational selfie, openly examining the effects of your thinking and your behavior, having an open mind to new perspectives, discussing what you would otherwise keep to yourself, looking into more effective alternatives together.

A final thought for managers

Change leadership requires you to look at how you are unwittingly causing employee passivity, tough-going changes, low energy, limited creativity, and lack of commitment. The thing is to suppress automatic behavior (temporarily) in difficult situations and to make conscious choices. If we let our autopilot do its thing, we will generally end up doing things that differ greatly from what we claim to intend to do, making us inconsistent and trapping us in recurring problems. The overriding instruction on how to break out of the cycle is this: dare to learn openly! Be curious about the (in)consistency of your actions! Because to learn is to change.

It should be noted, however, that 'leadership' is a confusing concept. Our idea of leadership is often based on several subconscious assumptions that have formed over time, but which can get in our way. In fact, these assumptions are what lead us to experience more pressure, hence triggering our autopilot.

We all know that many of our assumptions are no good and irrational, but be honest, which of the following convictions influence your behavior?

✗ As the manager, I am my employees' superior; I can't let them walk all over me.

✗ As the manager, I have to make the right decisions and present a certain image.

✗ As the manager, I can't just admit to finding something difficult or having doubts; this would erode my authority.
✗ As the manager, I cannot openly learn, I have to show that I am competent and not out of my depth in my job.
✗ As the manager, I am responsible for keeping my people motivated.

These assumptions all fit into the unilateral control approach. Although it is a valid approach, we now know what the consequences are. It reduces the value you add as a manager. If you really want to help create a climate of change and learning, you are really going to have to put convictions such as those listed above to bed. Young professionals entering the labor market today will be happy to help you with that. This is a generation of professionals with hierarchy aversion, who see through hidden agendas and will ask direct questions to get to the bottom of what is really going on.

I wish you all the best in your journey of learning and change!

Breakthrough 15

What are your views on leadership?
The word leadership is often a misnomer. Our notions of what a leader should be and do can get in our way.
Write down the notions you foist on yourself in your role as leader.
❏ Which notions help you create a climate of open learning and change?
❏ Which notions stand in the way of such an open climate?

Create room for yourself by picking what you think are the five most important notions of leadership and stick to them. Call it 'my guideline for learning leadership.'

In the following I will give you an example.

My guideline for learning leadership

1. I am not always effective. It is okay for others to know about my errors or mistakes.
2. Others have valuable information about the effects of my approach and behavior.
3. I know only part of the relevant information. Together with others, I can complete the picture.
4. If the process stagnates, the key lies in the here and now.
5. I will take a picture of the situation and make sure I am in it: how am I perpetuating the difficult situation?

Start small

1. *A climate of learning and change is not something you can implement.*
2. *Start small, examine your effectiveness, experiment, and learn. Make sure you do this openly.*
3. *If you keep evaluating challenging meetings to examine your behavior, you will eventually develop an ability to catch yourself out whenever you adopt defensive behavior. If you are then able to intervene and disable your defensive reflex, you have made it into the elite.*
4. *Leading change is a continuous learning process: stay alert to inconsistency between what you say and what you do.*

Personal message to the reader

Dear Reader,

Thank you for reading this book to the end. Although I have taken great pleasure in writing this book, there is also something about it that sits somewhat uneasy with me. As the reader, you take note of my ideas, but I do not know who you are, what you think about the subjects covered in this book, and what thoughts you had while reading this book. This makes writing a one-way street.

Thankfully, we live in an age where it does not have to be. I would like to hear from you. I want to personally invite you to join the network that I am building around the contents of this book. Go to *www.doorbreekdecirkel.nl* and sign up as a member.

Signing up will give you access to resources and opportunities to get in touch with me and others. This includes:
- practical cases with interaction options
- opportunities to present your cases to others and to me
- registration for workshops about the book
- the research on which the book is based
- videos with interviews about *Break the Cycle!*

I promise that I will personally reply to any questions you want to put to me and that have emerged from your day-to-day practices.

Kind regards, Arend Ardon

changestudio.nl
arend@changestudio.nl
www.linkedin.com/in/arendardon/

Sources of inspiration

In this section of the book, I would like to share some of my sources of inspiration with you, authors who inspired me in writing this book.

Chris Argyris

My main source of inspiration. His books are, in a word, masterly, although they are by no means easy reads. It would sometimes take me a week to get through five pages and properly grasp the implications of what I was reading. Concepts such as unilateral control and defensive behavior were derived from the works of Chris Argyris. His *Overcoming Organizational Defenses* is a real must-read in my view, provided you can deal with a little complexity.

Peter Senge

Peter Senge rose to fame with his book *The Fifth Discipline*, which made the concept of thinking in systematic patterns (such as vicious cycles) accessible to a broader public. I read this book in one go, I simply could not put it down. He also co-authored another equally magnificent book, *Presence*.

Bill Noonan

Bill Noonan and I have something in common. We have both set out to make Argyris' work accessible. Noonan also focuses on vicious cycles. His *Discussing the Undiscussable* offers a wide range of tools and short checklists. The accompanying DVD with interviews makes this book extra powerful.

Diana McLain Smith

For many years, Diana McLain Smith worked together with Argyris. In her work, she shows beautifully how recurring patterns shape relationships. Her recent book, *Divide or Conquer*, provides a detailed step-by-step plan for analysis of such patterns.

Roger Schwarz

Roger Schwarz's work is primarily about applying Argyris' insights to how teams work. His book, *The Skilled Facilitator* details possible interventions to boost team performance.

Karl Weick and Robert Quinn

In 1999, they published a groundbreaking article in *Annual Review of Psychology* that inspired me enormously: 'Organizational change and development.' This article is all about the difference between episodic change and continuous change.

Break the Cycle! is based on my PhD thesis, *Moving Moments*. Needless to say, I have used many more sources for my thesis, so this brief outline of my sources of inspiration is by no means exhaustive.

About the author

"It is my passion to, together with clients, explore new ways, make change inspirational, and set things in motion. I believe that innovation is achieved only through innovative methods and that inspiration is created only through inspiring interventions. We have some fine challenges ahead of us!"

Dr. Arend J. Ardon (1967) has a degree in both social psychology and business administration. He is founder of The Change Studio – Lead. Inspire. Create. It is his passion to, together with clients, make change inspirational, set things in motion, and explore new ways. This sometimes involves exposing and breaking out of well-worn patterns to be able to pick up the pace of change. Arend likes to be closely involved in innovation processes, often supported by his team of highly experienced change coaches.

Common requests that he gets from clients include:

- 'Help us shape a beautiful and inspiring change process.'
- 'Help us understand why we are having so much trouble getting change off the ground; help us break out of the cycle.'

- 'Help us bolster our people's entrepreneurial spirit or customer focus.'
- 'How can we as a company up our game when it comes to innovation?'
- 'Help us bring to life our strategy.'
- 'We want to launch a leadership process to learn together with our managers how to support the new course with our behavior.'
- 'Design and facilitate a memorable leadership journey for us.'

Arend teaches at various business schools, including Maastricht University's School of Business and Economics, where he holds a senior lectureship. Besides being a sought-after conference and seminar speaker, he also gives presentations as part of in-company programs on a regular basis.

Ardon has published dozens of articles and several books, including *Klantgestuurde teams*, *Veranderen spiegelen aan anderen*, *Klantleren*, *Duurzaam veranderen* (co-author) and *Essentie van leiderschap* (co-author). His strong desire to understand 'what is really happening here' was the driving force behind his doctoral thesis entitled *Moving Moments; Leadership and Interventions in Dynamically Complex Change Processes*, which earned him a doctorate from VU University Amsterdam in 2009.
He does not only work in the Netherlands, but is also invited by companies in other countries, such as the Netherlands Antilles, Great Britain, Denmark, Finland, Belgium, Sweden, Oman, Singapore, and Suriname.

Appendices

Break the Cycle! - The Six Principles at a glance

by Arend Ardon

Principle 1 Recognize persistent situations

1. When things get difficult and your best intentions do not lead to improvement: stop!
2. More of the same will only get you into more trouble.
3. You've got no time to lose, so explore how the same problems keep recurring.
4. Take a picture of the situation and make sure you are in it: how are you perpetuating the unwanted situation?

Principle 2 Be aware of your thinking about change

1. Your subconscious assumptions about change drive your choices in defining a change approach. Know your assumptions!
2. If you think that only you can initiate change and that employees do not want to change, you will eventually be right.
3. Structures and systems can be implemented, but behavior and attitude are things that you have to learn together.
4. When things become difficult, take a look at interactions in the here and now; they are the key.

Principle 3 See what you do when the going gets tough

1. When the going gets tough, your autopilot tells you: make sure you stay in control!
2. Without realizing it, you pile on the pressure, try to convince others, and disregard inconvenient information.
3. This is how you, unwittingly and without realizing it, produce unwanted effects. Others say 'yes,' think 'no,' and disengage.
4. Effective change is to learn what behavior and/or what thinking could breathe new life into the situation.

Principle 4 Understand how you are perpetuating the situation

1. If you feel you are going around in circles, you probably are: vicious cycles.
2. Your preconceptions of the other make you selective in what you see. This is how you create your own confirmation.
3. Vicious cycles have a self-protection mechanism: you keep pushing each other back into old habits.
4. To stop the hamster wheel, you need to learn together: how are we keeping each other trapped in this situation and how could we do things differently?

Principle 5 Dare to discuss the undiscussable

1. Information about our ineffectiveness is inconvenient and will make us go on the defensive.
2. We keep painful information under wraps by using defensive strategies, such as the downplay strategy and the humor strategy.
3. Only after repeatedly highlighting defensive behavior will these strategies start to weaken and give way to learning and change.
4. There is an art to making the undiscussable discussable: stay neutral in identifying behavior, effects, and inconsistency.

Principle 6 Start small

1. A climate of learning and change is not something you can implement.
2. Start small, examine your effectiveness, experiment and learn. Make sure you do this openly.
3. Conscious learning will ultimately enable you to catch yourself out and intervene whenever you adopt defensive behavior.
4. Leading change is a continuous learning process: stay alert to inconsistency between what you say and what you do.

Circular process charts

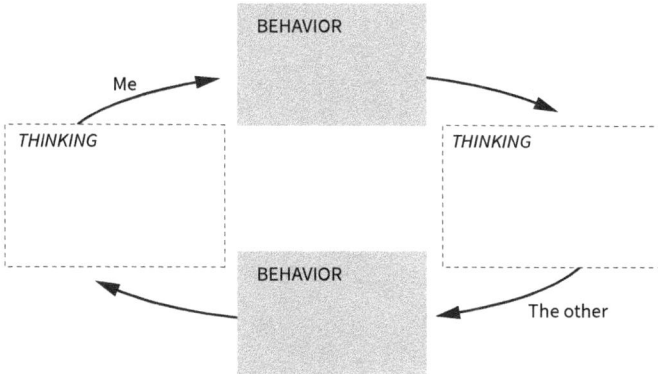

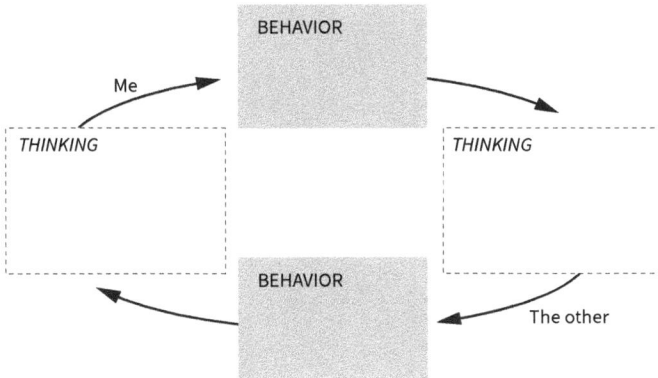

BEHAVIOR

Me

THINKING

THINKING

BEHAVIOR

The other

BEHAVIOR

Me

THINKING

THINKING

BEHAVIOR

The other

Defensive strategies scorecard

Bingo!

Situation: a team talk about a non-straightforward subject, such as the progress of the change process, team effectiveness, or the level of effort put in by individual team members.

Gameplay: all team members receive the below checklist with defensive strategies that people often use in team situations. Check the boxes for the defensive strategies you recognize. The idea is that as soon as a team member has checked three boxes, they shout 'bingo!' The game is then paused to allow this team member to present their observations.

❏ The pass-the-buck strategy
Whenever your approach/behavior turns out to be ineffective, blame it on circumstances and/or someone else.

❏ The downplay strategy
Whenever a situation becomes threatening or awkward, downplay the problem to make it manageable again.

❏ The we strategy
Keep the conversation impersonal by speaking in terms of 'our responsibility' and 'what we must do.'

❏ The evasion strategy
When a discussion comes too close to home, change the subject to other people or general observations, such as employees, middle management, or the company.

❏ The non-intervention strategy
Don't mention the ineffectiveness of others, so they won't mention yours either.

❏ The humor strategy
When a situation becomes threatening or awkward, crack a joke and change the subject

www.ingramcontent.com/pod-product-compliance
Lightning Source LLC
Chambersburg PA
CBHW071154200326
41519CB00018B/5222